Resisting Empire

The Book of Revelation as Resistance

C. Wess Daniels

BARCLAY
PRESS

Resisting Empire
The Book of Revelation as Resistance

©2019 C. Wess Daniels
Barclay Press, Inc.
Newberg, OR 97132
www.barclaypress.com

All rights reserved. No part may be reproduced for any commercial purpose by any method without permission in writing from the copyright holder.

Scripture quotations are from New Revised Standard Version Bible, copyright © 1989 National Council of the Churches of Christ in the United States of America. Used by permission. All rights reserved worldwide.

Cover and interior design: Mareesa Fawver Moss
Cover photo: Rob Potter
ISBN 978-1-59498-063-3

To the Quaker congregation known as
Camas Friends Church, may your lampstand
continue to embody the prophetic, participatory, and
inclusivity worthy of the Lamb that was slain.

Contents

7	Let Us Be the Ones
9	Acknowledgments
13	Foreword
19	Introduction: Revelation, Resistance, and the End of the World
33	Chapter 1: Some Strategies for Reading the Bible with Liberation, Imagination, and Empathy
47	Chapter 2: From Bafflement to Wonder (Revelation 1)
59	Chapter 3: Light Walking Around (Revelation 2–3)
67	Chapter 4: The Lamb that Was Slain (Revelation 5)
81	Chapter 5: Finding Our New Song (Revelation 7)
87	Chapter 6: Resistance Is the Work of the People (Revelation 12)
97	Chapter 7: The Multitude (Revelation 7)

105	Chapter 8: Economics, Poverty, and Crashing the Beast's Party (Revelation 13, 18)
117	Chapter 9: Revelation Is Remix (Revelation 21–22)
127	And in the End
129	Afterword
133	Endnotes

Let Us
Be the Ones

be not made to fear your voice
your seed
love wrested forward
raced

instinct primæval has in us since
immemorial
time-dreamed us
in a word.

saw-me-saw-you-in-one-word.
unique.
you. it is your word indeed
we need

now you. be not
made to fear
your one & only voice
no

let us be the ones.

—Rashaun Phillip Sourles
@Rashaunps (Me/Him)

Acknowledgments

This book is the result of my personal growth, an awakening really, that was brought on by new perspectives and shifting metaphors and language, not only for understanding and interpreting Scripture, but for understanding and relating to God. Upon becoming a pastor of a Quaker meeting in the Pacific Northwest in 2009, my theology began to undergo dramatic and necessary changes. I was living out the title of James Alison's book, *Undergoing God*. Still fresh in my doctoral program, my head was full of theory; my heart was searching. The result of becoming a "released minister," as it is sometimes called in Quaker circles, meant that praxis led to a reformulation of theory. There are a number of key people, communities, and events that helped me rethink my understanding of Revelation.

My two friends, Rev. Shelly Fayette and Aaron Scott, introduced me to new and challenging perspectives on identity and understanding the Bible. They also introduced me to the Poverty Initiative—Kairos Center—at Union Theological Seminary. A weekend seminar I participated in on Strategies for Reading the Bible in light of Liberation Theology and Anti-Poverty work produced a fundamental shift in the way I read the Bible and practice my faith. I have Shelly and Aaron to thank for inviting me to that weekend, but even more than that, for all the guest lectures, sermons, Bible studies, and conversations that supported my growth. I want to also thank Willie Baptist, Colleen Wessel-McCoy, John Wessel-McCoy, Liz Theoharis, Crystal Hall, and other Poverty Initiative Scholars whose ideas helped to shape and guide the creation of this book. I hope that what is reflected here is faithful to the gifts you have offered me.

This book is a tapestry, weaving together a series of reflections that have taken shape over a number of years. It started out as a series of sermons that I shared with Camas Friends Church in Camas, Washington. Then I delivered versions of these talks and developed new content for Quaker yearly meetings and churches, as well as for a Cooperative Baptist church in town. Lastly, to the students of the Quaker Leadership Scholar Program at Guilford College, where I most recently shared these ideas. Here was a group of college students willing to give Revelation a chance and see what it might offer them. I was delighted by your passion around this topic and the creative ways you interpreted it for your own lessons that you shared back with the rest of class. Therefore, I want to acknowledge all of these congregations, communities, and Guilford students who wrestled with these teachings with me—who asked hard questions, challenged particular interpretations, and lit up with passion at the idea that Revelation might be about something radically different from being left behind.

Thank you to Wes Howard-Brook (for your scholarship, witness, and foreword!), Elisabeth Schüssler Fiorenza, James Cone, bell hooks, Dorothee Sölle, Ched Myers, Bayard Rustin, James Alison, Zachary Moon, Peggy Morrison and Alivia Biko, Rev. Dr. William J. Barber II, T. Vail Palmer Jr., and many others whose work impacted this book and whose witness in this world compelled me to write.

To Darryl Aaron for this powerful afterword (not to mention the friendship and keen pastoral eye on all matters of empire), Rashaun Sourles whose poetry is a gift to this world, and Barclay Press publishing this work.

Foreword

"And afterward,
I will pour out my Spirit on all people.
Your sons and daughters will prophesy,
your old men will dream dreams,
your young men will see visions.
²⁹ Even on my servants, both men and women,
I will pour out my Spirit in those days.
³⁰ I will show wonders in the heavens
and on the earth,
blood and fire and billows of smoke.
³¹ The sun will be turned to darkness
and the moon to blood
before the coming of the great and dreadful
day of the LORD.
³² And everyone who calls
on the name of the LORD WILL BE SAVED…

—Joel 2:28–32 (NIV)

Prophecies….dreams…visions…These are the ways that God, according to the prophet Joel, will reveal God's will for God's people in difficult times. They will not be announced by religious officials or the political elite, but by ordinary people, both young and old, female and male, who identify as the "servants" of God.

The New Testament takes up this vision in the second half of the evangelist Luke's work, known as the Acts of the Apostles. In the mouth of an uneducated fisherman from the distant outpost of northern Galilee, Joel's ancient promise became enfleshed reality among the disciples of the crucified and risen Jesus just as the Roman Empire was coming into its power in the mid-first century of the common era.

The prophet-visionary of the late first century known as "John of Patmos" was among those Jesus-followers who received and proclaimed a prophetic vision from God. The text that contains his vision closes the biblical collection: the book of Revelation.

As Wess Daniels names at the outset of his delightful little introduction to this final biblical text, no other book has been as consistently and wildly misread as has John of Patmos's visionary narrative. And yet, at the same time, no biblical book carries as much passionate power and imagery aimed at inspiring Jesus-followers to "come out" of the place of imperial violence and domination and to dwell instead in the light- and love-filled realm of God. So Wess masterfully and clearly lays out a series of reading strategies and perspectives culled from the best of recent scholarship to invite readers into engagement with John's vision. If you've been drawn to study Revelation but have been stymied as to where or how to start, you can trust Wess's step-by-step guidance to lead you into the depth and breadth of this unique narrative.

Both God and the devil are in the details of Revelation, as Wess knows. However, this book is not the kind of verse-by-verse commentary that can overwhelm beginners with mountains of data. Rather, Wess introduces readers to the core messages and basic themes around which the granular structure of John's vision is shaped.

Read within its first century cultural context and within what Wess calls a "remix" of ancient biblical imagery, there can be no doubt about John's message to the seven, little communities of Jesus-followers in the Roman province of Asia: God's call to "come out" of the "whore" of Babylon and to abide instead in God's open-doored, holy city, New Jerusalem. Those who have developed what Jesus calls "ears to hear" (e.g., Mark 4:9) will recognize "Babylon" as the biblical symbol of "the great city," the ancient label for what we today call "empire" (e.g., Genesis 10:12; Jonah 1:2; Revelation 11:8; 18:10ff). It is a realm grounded in fear that leads to violence, exclusion of others and radical economic inequality. In its place, God's people are exhorted to find our home in what the Gospels call "the realm of God," Martin Luther King, Jr. called "the Beloved Community," and John of Patmos calls "New Jerusalem." It is a city, not made by human labor via the accumulation of capital, but rather, given as a gift from God. It is the realm where love-in-community leads to abundance for all with God's vulnerable presence at the very center (e.g., Revelation 21).

Wess explores four themes that shape this message. They are:

1. *The role of "scapegoating"* as a means by which empires shift the blame from themselves to the other. Wess uses the seminal work of Rene Girard to trace how John's vision reveals the biblical theme of scapegoating at work in the empire.

2. *The critique of imperial economics,* through which empires establish and maintain wealth for the few at the expense of slavery and oppression for the masses of poor people. Here we see how

slave-based exploitation of God's creation—including human beings—is the foundation for the corrupt economics that the empire would claim is "the gift of the gods."

3. *The competing "liturgies"* by which "Babylon" and "New Jerusalem" beckon people to express their loyalty to one way of life or the other. Wess here highlights the twin call of church worship to express enthusiastic resistance to the claims of empire *and* celebration of the Victory of God's true agent of peace and salvation, Jesus, the Lamb of God.

4. *The symbol of "the multitude" as a celebration of an alternative social order,* where people pushed to the margins of imperial society are now found at the center. In place of the rigid, Roman social hierarchy, we discover the multicultural multitude that gathers around the throne of the Lamb as a community of mutual love for all creation.

Wess weaves his exposition from a wide variety of conversational threads, including leading biblical scholars, revered elders from Wess's Quaker tradition, committed faith-activists of color, and myriad pop culture figures and works. In other words, his book is "remixed" much as John's Revelation is, with its references to the world of first century Rome and endless echoes of sacred stories from the deep past of the Bible. Both John and Wess thereby help their respective readers to hear that God's message remains the same then and now, despite empire's shape-shifting and name-changing over the eons. Whether the Rome of John's time or the faceless global empire of our own day, God's people remain called to leave behind the realm of violence, hatred, and poverty for our true home where the peace of the Lamb reigns over all creation (Revelation 5).

As a good teacher and a humble disciple of Jesus, Wess rightly refrains from offering a fix to the problem. Rather, in good Quaker fashion, he leaves it to communities of readers to listen for the Spirit's guidance in our own contexts. Just as John addressed unique words of comfort and challenge to each of the seven communities his vision addresses, Wess knows that readers of this book must seek our own way out of empire in the specific places where God's Word finds us.

One can easily read this book in a few hours. Living out its hopeful message is the work of a lifetime. With climate change's devastating impact accelerating each day and year, with increasingly widespread calls around the world for walls and tightened borders against desperate refugees, the time to begin that work is *now*. May this book bless those who seek God's liberating and empowering Word with inspiration and clarity as we walk together on the Way of Jesus, out of the domination and death of empire and into the light and abundant life of God's glorious realm.

—Wes Howard-Brook

Introduction
Revelation, Resistance, and the End of the World

[The Bible is...] a collection of stories of poor people uniting across difference to build a social movement and winning.
—Rev. Dr. Liz Theoharis

So much damage has been done in the name of the Bible, and specifically, the book of Revelation. There is a clear and mainstream reading of Revelation that says it is all about the end of the world. I want to offer an alternative reading, and I believe this alternative is so dramatically different from our assumptions that it will shock you. Look around. If we are to stand up to empire in our own time, we need to be shocked out of the comfort of our Western Christian assumptions.

Here's the deal: Revelation speaks to the reality that we are caught in the fray of cosmic conflict. We are guilty. We've already been contaminated. But it's not too late for us to exit empire and enter the kingdom. We are yet both victim and victimizer. We have healing work to do, and we must take responsibility for the ways in which we have benefited from and been complicit with the religion of empire.

This is the truth of Revelation. God wants to liberate us in body, heart, soul, and mind. We need rescue. But we don't know we need rescue. Empire is not just something I participate in with a vote or a war tax; it is a whole way of thinking, acting, and worshiping in the world. It surrounds us.

The way we read Revelation determines how we define ourselves and our communities in relation to empire and in resistance to it. Reading Revelation as Western Christians have over the past 150 years or so, as a book predicting the end of the world, leads us into territories that take us away from what I believe is the book's original intention. These interpretations are not your typical beautiful-prince-marries-mermaid-princess fairy-tale endings, either. It is always based on some people winning and many others facing destruction. Have you noticed that the people explaining the meaning of Revelation are always on the winning team? Or how the people they don't like always end up on the punishing side of God's wrath. It's awfully convenient theology.

But besides using the Bible book to create "us" and "them" categories, the other thing that these interpreters of Revelation have done is to argue for "evacuation theology." Revelation (and let's face it, plenty of other texts in the Bible as well) are interpreted along the lines of rapture and escape.

It's irresponsible. When we're only interested in how we might evacuate a planet in crisis, abstracting ourselves from politics, avoiding responsibility for people—we expose ourselves as Christians who don't care, who don't love, who don't look much like Jesus. We know this all too well. Revelation has been used to justify this kind of thinking: "Why bother, really? The world is already burning."

Let's start over.

The Lenses We Bring

I'm an oldest child. I'm a white, male, cisgender heterosexual. I have an education. But I also grew up in a working class family. My mom and step-dad both dropped out of high school, and while they valued education for their six children, they themselves did not have access to the kinds of resources that many take for granted. These are just some of the lenses I bring to my reading of the Bible, and when I read it I cannot get away from the fact that these things are there in my reading and interpretation. Having lenses is normal. There's nothing wrong with seeing what I see, as long as I know that's not all there is—as long as I value (and learn from) what others with different experiences can see that I can't. I read any text first for experiences that match and sound like mine. This is an unconscious and natural way to read. I connect with what I know, with what's familiar. Conscious reading requires that I also interrogate my reading, asking, What am I bringing to the text? What am I reading into the text that may not really be there? Are there certain aspects of the text and its stories that I am giving too much attention to while overlooking other experiences, perspectives, and stories that the text wants to make me aware of? Also, these lenses we employ while reading can be both positive and negative. I have plenty of students who come to class with negative experiences of the Bible. We all start from wherever we are. My hope is that, over time, we might move into the imaginative—even the scholarly—work necessary to see the text anew, looking for new experience, open to new perspectives and possibilities.

The biblical text also has its own lenses that it brings to us. The Bible is not one book. It is like an ancient Kindle, a small portable library full of poetry, letters, stories, and more. Each of these texts has its own lenses and experiences with which it comes to us. In other words, not only do we read the text, but the text also reads us. And we have to negotiate the tension between these two experiences. Are we aware of what those lenses are, what aspects, perspectives, cultural issues, and challenges these ancient books were trying to address? Who wrote them, and who were they written too? I don't just mean, who was the person—or people—who wrote a book like Exodus, but what was their social location? Did they have particular identities (race, gender, class, sexuality, religion) that would help us understand their experiences and perspectives? Have we done, or are we willing to do, the reading and studying necessary to become more aware? In the same way that one might attend a lecture on Melville's *Moby Dick* or an upper level seminar on Shakespearean texts from just a few hundred years ago, a text that is more than two thousand years old requires us to do a lot of work to begin to understand the rich tapestry of meaning we find there.

We have this idea within American Christianity that we can just show up to the text, read it, and understand it. Sometimes we chalk our understanding up to the Holy Spirit. Often though, if we're honest, it's mostly just our own biases that we're unconsciously reading into the text. I have no doubt the Holy Spirit helps us to read and understand texts—especially when we read in community. But it is far too easy to credit the Holy Spirit with our individual understandings when we also need to check our understandings with the larger community and denominational structures to which we find ourselves accountable. I also want to say, however, that it has been rare that the Holy Spirit has taught me about the specifics of a particular Greek word and the difference it can make in an interpretation; nor has the Holy Spirit illuminated for me the intricacies of the practice of say, first century, Jewish marriage rituals. I suppose the Holy Spirit can do this kind of teaching, but also, there are plenty of Christian pastors, scholars, and activists who have already done this work for us. Rather, my experience has been more that the Holy Spirit's role helps the discerning interpreter of the text read it in light of their particular community and its needs today. What does this text have to say to us today? We need to know what it meant to the people who originally wrote it and read it before we can get to this second question because we know that we are not the intended audience of any of the books of the Bible. Understanding this truth opens up the text, under the guidance of the Spirit, to establish its ongoing relevance for us today as a *living text*.

Therefore, I have hinted at least one more layer to keep in front of us, and that is the lens of our particular faith community, how that community reads and is shaped by the text. Each community and each community's tradition operates as an interpretive framework. If I am an Evangelical Christian in Ohio, my community may interpret the book of Revelation very differently from Black Pentecostal Christians in the South, who may very well interpret the text differently from Quakers living in Kenya, or Catholic farmers in South America.

Four Themes of Revelation

Before we move into the main content of this book, I want to outline four main themes of the book of Revelation. I am sure there are other themes and that other scholars highlight different aspects of the text. Here I am lifting up what I see to be the key threads that deal with a text concerned with resisting empire.

The four themes that will be woven throughout the rest of this book are: Revelation reveals how scapegoating functions within empire to define its own boundaries and contours as being over and against wicked others; Revelation critiques wealth and shows that even in the first century there was prophetic critique against an economic system that was based on abundance for some, while exploiting the rest; Revelation demonstrates the importance of liturgy as something that forms people into the likeness of either empire or the lamb; and finally, Revelation reveals an alternative social order which becomes the center of resistance rooted in a vision of what the book describes as "the multitude," and what I call, a community without antagonism. I will briefly describe each of these in turn.

1. Enemies and the Scapegoat Mechanism

If you grew up with younger siblings, like I did, the idea of scapegoating is almost intuitive. And even more so if you were a middle child. Let me ask you, when your older or younger siblings did something they shouldn't have done, what often happened to you? Did you manage to get blamed for the shenanigans of a sibling, a friend, or a classmate? Or maybe you were like I was as the oldest child—the one who got out of the hot seat because there was usually someone else around to take the fall.

My guess is that we all have examples from childhood where we were blamed for something we didn't do. I have heard it said, "That pain that is not transformed is transmitted," that we tend to take our deepest wounds and project them onto others rather than dealing with them ourselves. The Bible calls this scapegoating. Think about just a few examples:

- Eve has often been the scapegoat for the "fall" of humanity.
- If you were the child of divorced parents, you may have taken the blame for that.
- Maybe you lost a relationship or a job because you were scapegoated for something that you didn't do.

Where does this idea of scapegoat originate?

In the Old Testament, during the Jewish Day of Atonement, there was a goat offered for the people's sins. As strange as it may seem to us now, it was initially a kind of third way. The scapegoating allowed for a space in between you and me; it interrupted the cycle of violence. Instead of taking out my rage onto you for the hurt you caused me or my family, the priests would displace that rage into a scapegoat that they would then send out into the wilderness, relieving the tension that had been between us. It is also important to note that in the system laid out in Leviticus 16, the scapegoat was not to be killed.

Eventually, within the biblical tradition, John the Baptist calls Jesus the "lamb of God who takes away the sins of the world." Jesus becomes the once for all scapegoat meant to not only bring an end to this vicious cycle, but to reveal that the scapegoat is in fact innocent and that for real peace to be sustained, humanity needs to confront, head on, its pain and its hostility toward one another.

Viewed this way, Jesus' death reveals something deeply important about the image of God that much of humanity still works from. It is not God who is violent, seeking revenge and sacrifice; it is humanity that is blood thirsty and that uses scapegoating to sustain a modicum of peace.

James Alison points out the real kicker of Jesus as the lamb when he says, "It is not humans who sacrifice to God (by killing the blasphemous transgressor), it is God who offers a sacrifice to humans." This image of a violent God is the one we pass onto a lot of our young people. I have countless students who come to college saying they don't believe in God, but what they mean is that they don't believe in Zeus, a capricious and violent divine "father figure with a long white flowy beard."

René Girard, a French theorist, has developed the idea of how the scapegoat mechanism continues to work in our own society today, even though most of us aren't sacrificing animals regularly. The scapegoat mechanism lies at the very foundation of how our social order works.

Empires, so far as I can tell, have always relied heavily on the scapegoat mechanism. In order to create and maintain social control, there are social boundaries and identities that always play out as a rivalry between us and them. Empire needs the "them," the ones we can cast blame on, the ones we can point the finger at for any problems we may face, the ones who, even if they appear to have basic rights, are generally agreed upon in advance to not really have rights because they've been written off as "aliens" and therefore can't be a part of our covenanter community. It's relatively easy to expel them as needed.

I will develop this idea further throughout the following chapters, but scapegoating is an essential function that any chronically anxious system utilizes to stabilize power, and empires are no different in this way.

2. Imperial Economics

Throughout Revelation, there are countless places John critiques imperial economics, which I am defining as that which benefits some at the expense of the many. Revelation reveals that imperial economics is an entire system of oppression. It is not just a matter of one person not giving enough wealth away; it is a whole system bent on exploitation.

Revelation reveals that poverty, slavery, and exploitation of the earth's resources are not a sign of a broken system. The system is working just as it was designed. And this is the very thing that God threatens extremely harsh judgment upon.

As we will see later, in Revelation 18, there is a brilliant explication of God's preferential option for the poor and those crushed by empire. It clearly shows that God is not judging the city because of anything other than an unrighteousness that manifests itself in economic greed and exploitation.

3. The Two Liturgies of Empire and the Lamb

A third theme that arises throughout Revelation is that there are competing liturgies. Here we should think of liturgies as those practices, rituals, language, and symbols that shape us in particular ways and for particular ends. Revelation warns us that empire has its own liturgy. Empire's ceremonies create an atmosphere of worship that draws people into a particular narrative. It dulls the senses and forms a kind of alienation over time that keeps people from challenging its ideology.

Wes Howard-Brook writes that "this war took the form of ritual crucifixions, arena contests with lions, and other public spectacles of execution. John's insight is that these are not merely 'political' acts, but liturgical acts as well...[Even] 'the courtrooms with the robed magistrates, the choreographed rising and sittings, collective responses and other ritual acts' are all a part of this 'liturgical demeanor.'" On the one hand, the empire's religion of temples, statutes, decrees, ordinances, and symbols are for John a kind of liturgy that dulls the hearts and minds of its subjects. This liturgy is meant to abstract you from the present moment, lull you to sleep so that you are not awake to your own suffering—let alone the suffering of your neighbor. To participate in the liturgy of empire is to be unable to see the ways in which we are both agents and targets of oppression.

On the other hand, there is a second competing liturgy in Revelation and that is the liturgy of *the lamb that was slain*, one that is rooted in non-violence, in love of neighbor and enemy, and understands God to be for all of creation. This liturgy builds resilience, shapes theological imaginations in ways that people can have the antibodies necessary to resist empire, and it is truthful—it helps us to see where we are complicit with empire and how we might begin to subvert it. Each liturgy reveals the image of God behind it—one a god of violence and the other a God of love.

James Cone, in *The Cross and the Lynching Tree*, describes the ways in which a lynching of African-Americans, often by white Christians, functioned very much like a kind of twisted church service. Liturgy, whether it is a political rally, a mass, or a silent meeting, can be used for positive or negative formation of people. It can dull the heart, stunt the imagination, and make us content with the way things are. Even worse, it can lead us to do horrific things in the name of God.

Or liturgy can slowly over time rebuild us from the inside out, free us from what binds us, and lead us into a liberatory life and language that dismantles oppression and harmful systems in this world. Revelation not only helps me in my critique of the system out there, but it requires that I reflect on the ways in which I am being caught up in worship and formation of the wrong gods.

I'm not even sure if I should mention the political landscape today: the infighting, the victim-blaming, the attack ads, the scapegoating. This is all the liturgy of empire made manifest before our very eyes. It thrives off rallying us against one another, building up to a sacrifice. It all sounds so much like a public spectacle of execution.

The counter to this is Christian worship that forms us into living in ways that are meant to be public spectacles of life and caregiving.

I like how James Alison describes an alternative liturgy that might begin to form us in ways that resist the frenzy we love to get caught up in:

> When people tell me they find Mass boring, I want to say to them: it's supposed to be boring, or at least seriously underwhelming. It's a long-term education in becoming unexcited, since only that will enable us to dwell in a quiet bliss which doesn't abstract from our present or our sounding or our neighbor, but which increases our attention, our presence and our appreciation for what is around us. The build-up to a sacrifice is exciting, the dwelling gratitude that the sacrifice has already happened, and that we've been forgiven for and through it [and therefore have no more need of sacrifice or scapegoats] is, in terms of excitement, a long drawn-out let-down.[1]

4. The Multitude: An Alternative Social Order

This brings me to one final and very powerful image within Revelation, and that is the image of the multitude. In contrast to the religion of empire—creating social hierarchies and persisting in violence through the scapegoat mechanism—is this image of people in worship, gathered around the lamb:

> Revelation 7: 9 After this I looked, and there was a great multitude that no one could count, from every nation, from all tribes and peoples and languages, standing before the throne and before the Lamb, robed in white, with palm branches in their hands. 10 They cried out in a loud voice, saying, "Salvation belongs to our God who is seated on the throne, and to the Lamb!" 11 And all the angels stood around the throne and around the elders and the four living creatures, and they fell on their faces before the throne and worshiped God, 12 singing, "Amen! Blessing and glory and wisdom and thanksgiving and honor and power and might be to our God forever and ever! Amen."

The multitude is a beautiful tapestry woven together of all humanity, with those who were lynched, those who were oppressed and victimized, at the center with the lamb. This centering of the victims and marginalized is something that is too often missed within Western, white, middle-class Christianity today. This centering of those on the margins is made explicit in this next passage from Chapter 7, which also leads into one of the most powerful passages of Revelation:

13 Then one of the elders addressed me, saying, "Who are these, robed in white, and where have they come from?" 14 I said to him, "Sir, you are the one that knows." Then he said to me, "These are they who have come out of the great ordeal; they have washed their robes and made them white in the blood of the Lamb. 15 For this reason they are before the throne of God, and worship him day and night within his temple, and the one who is seated on the throne will shelter them. 16 They will hunger no more, and thirst no more; the sun will not strike them, nor any scorching heat; 17 for the Lamb at the center of the throne will be their shepherd, and he will guide them to springs of the water of life, and God will wipe away every tear from their eyes."

We have here in the book of Revelation a very powerful image of the radical hospitality and inclusivity, the kind of vision which Martin Luther King Jr. would later call *the beloved community*. And for those of you who know your Bible, you know that this thread that becomes the multitude reaches back to the work of the Hebrew prophets who pushed their people to care for the victims, the poor, the aliens and strangers in their midst; it caught momentum in the ministry of Jesus who invested his time and healing efforts at the margins of society. This building vision really catches steam in the book of Acts. First in Acts 2, there is a great diversity of people who are all baptized in the Holy Spirit, which allows for them to have a unity amidst their difference, and later in that chapter we learn what it looks like for them to be in community together. Then in Acts 10, Peter is told by God not to call anything profane that God has called sacred. We find in Revelation a vision that has been building steam over the course of the whole biblical narrative, moving toward this final vision of the multitude—a fully diverse, inclusive, and loving community of all creation.

My hope is that as you read what I have written here, reflecting on the book of Revelation and images it presents, that your hearts and imaginations will be revived, made more resilient and ever more focused on the needs of the world that surround us. Let us stop at nothing to make space for others and amplify the voices of those whom the powers and principalities wish to silence. And in the end, you will find that you have already, always, been on the inside of the multitude, surrounding the lamb of God.

Chapter 1
Some Strategies for Reading the Bible with Liberation, Imagination, and Empathy

Before we turn to key themes in the book of Revelation, I want to say something about the role of imagination and empathy in how we read the text. I have been influenced by Quaker theologian and scholar T. Vail Palmer Jr., who argues that early Quakers read the Bible with empathy. That is, early Friends read the Bible as though they themselves were inside the story. Being able to do this well involves everything I mentioned earlier, as well as imagination and creativity. Inasmuch as we are able to read with empathy, we are open to new insight, differing interpretations, and creative uses of the text. To read in this way truly allows for the text to remain alive within our day and time. James Alison captures this perfectly:

> Imagine two different groups of scientists. One group, armed with a set of encyclopedic guidebooks which are constantly being annotated, take turns to look at a distant star or galaxy through an extremely powerful telescope. The scientists offer comments from what they see, and in the light of what they see, or deduce, further annotations are made in the guidebooks, and their deliverances are

passed on to anyone who is interested. The other group of scientists is standing round the rim of a huge concavity in the surface of the earth, or maybe there are in submarines, gazing at the rim of a huge concavity which has been detected as giving form to the sea bed. They are trying to work out what has happened, what force, what dimensions, what speed, produced this impact, and what the consequences have been, or are, or will be, for life on the planet as a result of whatever it was that produced this concavity.

Of the two groups of scientists, the one which offers the closer analogy to the discipline of theology is the second group. For the discipline of theology, a distinctively Christian discipline, presupposes a happening, an impact, an interruption, having already happened, and offering a shape which can be detected as the consequences of its having happened spread further. Furthermore, it presupposes that that happening, that impact, is not only a blind collision, of the sort produced by a meteor in the vicinity of the Yucatan peninsula, but is an act of communication. This means that the theologian is not merely an outsider, commenting about something having happened, but is on the way to becoming part of the act of communication from the inside. Is on the way to becoming a shock wave from the impact, which is part of the impact itself.[2]

Here Alison is writing specifically about the discipline of theology, but I want to be clear that while many of us do not think of ourselves as theologians, whenever we read and seek to interpret and put into practice the teachings of our sacred texts, we are doing theology. Alison's analogy here points out two very distinct ways of approaching the text. What do you notice about these two ways? What stands out to you about the second set of scientists? How might reading the Bible more in line with the second group change our approach and understanding of the text? This second approach is far more participatory and anticipatory. Not only does it include us in the story, we are the ones who are "becoming part of the act of communication from the inside," but it also anticipates that there will be new things to learn, new ways to grow and to understand.

I believe that what Alison is pointing to here is not unlike what early Quakers were trying to do with their reading of the Bible as well:

> As far as possible, Fox and Burrough were indeed thinking with Paul, John, and Luke; they had entered sympathetically and imaginatively into the New Testament community and were reliving its sacred history. Furthermore, they were expecting and assuming that their Quaker readers were likewise standing within the Bible—within the thought and life-world of the earliest Christians—and were looking out as the world through the window of biblical faith.
>
> For Fox and Fell, the biblical history was indeed the history of their own time; every player in the drama of seventeenth-century

England had a counterpart in the biblical drama of the people of God and its enemies.[3]

And Jon Kershner, a Quaker historian: "For early Quakers, the Bible was not just a bunch of stories about things that happened 2,000 years ago—the words of the Scriptures came alive and were fulfilled in their own lives. Howgill and the other early Quakers believed that the message of the Scriptures was a type of experience that would be embodied and reenacted in the lives of the faithful. As the Spirit applied the Scriptures to their lives, the early Quakers discerned God's will for them." An empathic reading of the Bible is less interested in reading the Bible for information and is more interested in reading it for inspiration. Those attempting to read the Bible with empathy will ask, "What is the text doing?" rather than, "What does it mean?"

As Eugene Peterson writes,

> When we approach the biblical text, instead of asking, "What does it mean?"—which is what people usually do—we should ask, "What is it doing? How do I enter into this? How does it enter into me?"
>
> You know, it's surprising: We have Jesus as the centerpiece of what we're doing, but he almost never talked in terms of explaining. He was always using enigmatic stories and difficult metaphors. He was always pulling people into some kind of participation.
>
> It's essential for us to develop an imagination that is participatory. Art is the primary way in which this happens. It's the primary way in which we become what we see or hear.

I think a pastor is in a unique position to cultivate this participatory imagination. We shouldn't just be giving information, because so much of what we're dealing with is entangled with the invisible, the inaudible, the unsayable.[4]

Four Strategies

While I am very interested in this idea of reading with empathy, it took me some time to work out for myself what it actually looks like to do this. Four ways to read the Bible with empathy are: reading off-center, tapestry, remix, and reenactment.

Off-Center

To read off-center is to attempt to read from a different perspective. We read off-center when we look for or listen to the marginalized position in the text. We look for the minor keys in the text, the people who are silenced, or whose voices are usually not amplified either in the text or by preachers and theologians today.

Consider, for example, the resurrection account in John 20. We often orient the story around the two men, but to focus the camera in on Mary gives us a different perspective. The men run off; Mary lingers. When we read off-center, we see that Mary is the hero of the story—she is the first apostle, the first to witness to the resurrected Christ, and the first to be given the command to go and tell. But with so much focus on the men—because one of our lenses has been deeply shaped by patriarchy—we lose this far more subversive element that the text is trying to point out to us.

Another example is in the book of Exodus, a powerful narrative about how God liberates God's people from oppressive regimes. We read that God liberated the Hebrews and automatically think this is the Jewish people; well not quite, at least not yet. The word "Hebrew" literally means marginalized, the oppressed. They were not one people group yet but a collection of people taken captive by the Egyptian empire and enslaved. It is in God's liberation of them from empire that they become a people.

Elisabeth Schüssler Fiorenza, a biblical scholar, applies this kind of thinking to Revelation (and is one of the key people I draw my framework from for this book) arguing that Revelation has itself been read from the margins:

> The next reading strategy searches through the Bible and Revelation for a language of hope and a paradigm of liberation from a world of poverty and oppression.[5]

The book of Revelation is about how to survive empire, or in modern parlance, how to stick it to the man. We have to understand that a lot of the Bible was written by people who were on the margins, people whose lived reality was nothing like our own. These are not people living comfortable, middle-class, American lives. These are the poor, the oppressed, the marginalized. How might you see and read the Bible differently if you realize that it is these voices that the texts are amplifying?

Schüssler Fiorenza argues that the Bible is a good text for the poor, and it encourages its readers to engage in the struggle for justice:

> In this course of action the reading becomes an act of interpreting "the oppressive powers of the present in light of the past and the future in light of God's liberating action. Such a

strategy for reading Revelation seeks to offer not only a way for understanding and naming the powers of evil but also a vision of justice and well-being that motivates the reader to engage in resistance and struggle for change.[6]

For example, Revelation chapters 13, 17–18, and 20–21, are well known to the poor of Central and South America (11). Firoenza suggests that one reason these texts often lack power for us is because we are reading them from a position of power. Adopting a middle-class, privileged reading means we lack the experiences these texts are talking about, and so we read them out of context.

Could it be that the people who feel particularly uncomfortable with the struggle in Revelation are the same people who experience discomfort acknowledging race, class, and privilege?

A really good challenge to our particular readings of Revelation is Martin Luther King Jr.'s *Letter from a Birmingham Jail*. King's letter is a good use of this empathetic reading of scripture (because of the way he uses Revelation).

His outline on the margins of a newspaper, written from a prison cell, drew upon a similar structure to the book of Revelation:

> The ethics of Christian commitment, the judgment of God upon the dehumanizing power of White America; and finally, allusions to the New Jerusalem, echoing King's famous *I Have a Dream* speech.[7]

These all match key themes, and even the outline of the book of Revelation. Fiorenza writes,

King's indictment of racist, White America would be completely misunderstood [in his *Letter from a Birmingham Jail*] if it were construed as "hatred of civilization," or as "envy deficient of Christian love," or as psychological displacement and repression of the "will to power." To construe King's indictment as such would mean to adopt the perspective of well-to-do White Americans who do not experience the same harassment, malnutrition, drug threat, discrimination, despair, and murder that constitute the daily experience of the black underclass. If one has experienced the dehumanizing power of racism as a life-destroying, evil power, one will grasp Revelation's outcry for justice. In a context of oppression, Revelation's depiction of evil and judgment is not seen as a wishful projection of revenge and bliss that is engendered by the author's limited perception of reality. Rather, it is understood as an inspired promise of justice and liberation given to those who are now suffering from dehumanizing systems of oppression.[8]

To read off-center is to look for the subversive elements, the places where the text cries out for justice, where it is amplifying voices that are often the ones we least want to hear.

Tapestry

Another way to read with empathy is to look for the tapestry within a text. We look for the places where the author weaves the stories, images, language, and metaphors of the Bible in our own language. Again, consider Martin Luther King Jr.'s *I Have a Dream* speech. It draws on metaphors to establish common ground and to summon the authority of Christian justice tradition. Nancy Duarte, a communications specialist, points out the ways in which King weaves together different metaphors to draw in his hearers:

> King establishes common ground by referencing many spiritual hymns and Scripture familiar to the audience. He even rephrases a small sequence from Shakespeare: "This sweltering summer of the Negro's legitimate discontent will not pass until there is an invigorating autumn."[9]

This is taken from, "Now is the winter of our discontent"—a line from William Shakespeare's *Richard III*. More lines from the speech are worth our time and attention:

> No, we are not satisfied, and we will not be satisfied until justice rolls down like waters, and righteousness like a mighty stream.
>
> That one day every valley shall be exalted, every hill and mountain shall be made low, the rough places will be made plain, and the glory of the Lord shall be revealed, and all flesh shall see it together.
>
> Free at last! Free at last! Thank God almighty, we are free at last!

Reading as tapestry is artful and invites participatory imagination. The hearers get to be in the know, especially when they get the reference. I think this is what Eugene Peterson means when he talks about participatory imagination.

You see something like this with George Fox and early Quakers as well. It is seen when they include biblical texts as if they are their own words (I've included them here to help you see what I mean):

> Sing and rejoice (Zachariah 2:10), you children of the day and of the light (1 Thessalonians 5:5); for the Lord is at work in this thick night of darkness that may be felt (Exodus 10:21). And truth does flourish as the rose (Isaiah 35:1), and the lilies do grow among the thorns (Song of Songs 2:1), and the plants atop of the hills (Jeremiah 31:3–5). And upon them the lambs do skip (Song of Songs 2:8) and play. -George Fox 1663 Epistle 227 (during a time of severe persecution of Quakers)

See how they weave in these texts—texts their readers would know well. This kind of tapestry not only pulls their readers into the story, but demonstrates how George Fox sees himself inside the story itself, quoting it as though its words are his words.

Remix

A third approach is what I call remix.

Remix is a method that reinvents something old by putting it into new language, new context, while honoring the spirit of the original.

Where do we see remix in today's world? There are so many examples. *Romeo and Juliet* by Baz Lurhmann; *Pride and Prejudice and Zombies* (Seth Grahame-Smith); the television show *Grimm* draws ideas from the old Brothers

Grimm fairy tales and re-presents them as part of a 21st century crime drama set in Portland, Oregon; the *West Side Story* is a classic example of remix. Fashion is always being remixed—in the 1990s, when I was in high school, my friends and I searched out local thrift shops, buying up all the old polyester shirts and velour suits. I had bell-bottoms I wore regularly, but then I'd add my own style, remixing it, so to speak. Of course, the whole concept of remix as we know it today comes from DJ culture.

Remix is a kind of dialogue with other texts:

> Fans poach, or remix, existing cultural material in a way that not only transgresses the text's original intent and blends it with other popular or traditional "texts," but also brings an authentic, self-expression to that material.
>
> Remix fosters interplay between one's own culture and the text.
>
> Remix is collage. It is legitimate derivative work that often challenges "the sanctioned expert interpretations and readings of the text."
>
> Remix is successful when it "leverages the meaning created by the reference to build something new."[10]

Remix is all through the Bible. For instance, in Acts 13, Paul begins to tell the story of Jesus' significance not with the resurrection, but with the beginning of Israel's story; but then he starts to change the ending, moving it toward Jesus, adding an alternative ending to how his hearers would have understood their history. This is a remix of history to point in a new direction, offering a reinterpretation that Paul believes is important to highlight and tell. Later we will look at an incredible example of remix found in Revelation 18.

One last example of remix comes from Quaker co-founder, Margaret Fell's early writing *Women's Speaking Justified*.

T. Vail Palmer Jr. points out that Fell's tract responds in depth to two key passages used against women speaking in church: 1 Corinthians 14:34–35 and 1 Timothy 2:11–12 (Palmer 2013: Chapter 2). Fell's closing line plays off the oft-quoted Pauline passage from 1 Timothy 2:11–12: "Let the woman learn in silence with all subjection. But I suffer not a woman to teach, nor to usurp authority over the man, but to be in silence" (KJV) by turning it back around on her opponents who she suggests should "remain silent." She remixes the biblical passage by saying, "So let all mouths be stopt that would limit him, whose Power and Spirit is infinite, that is pouring upon all flesh."

Fell's reinterpretation of the biblical text within her culture shows how it is possible to draw on original sources in new ways. By leveraging metaphors from Old Testament and New and appealing to the Spirit of God at work, she was able to put something new forward within Christianity. For Fell, "The biblical history was indeed the history of their own time; every player in the drama of 17th century England had a counterpart in the biblical drama of the people of God and its enemies."[11]

For those of you into improv, remix is a way of saying "yes, and…" of taking what is there and building upon it in order to see what comes out of it.

Re-enactment

This is what Quaker pastor and theological provocateur Peggy Morrison calls Godly Play for adults. Another way to read the Bible with empathy is to roleplay the story, to symbolize a message, or to act it out in some way. Even just acting out the movements of a story will often bring about a different perspective. Peterson Toscano, another Quaker who has influenced my thinking in this area, has a very powerful and well-done film titled *Transfigurations: Transgressing Gender in the Bible*, where he reenacts biblical stories off-center, looking for places where gender roles are challenged or transgressed in the Bible.

But also consider that the sit-ins, the Freedom Bus rides, and the marches during the Civil Rights movement were all acting out the biblical call toward justice. My favorite example of this was during the Poor People's Campaign of 1967 when there was a mule train that camped up from Marks, Mississippi, the place where Martin Luther King Jr. initially had the idea for the Poor People's Campaign after witnessing the astonishing poverty of that community. The people of Marks took a caravan of mules to D.C. to participate in the march and demonstrations. On the side of one wagon it said, "Don't laugh folks, Jesus was a poor man." Poor people riding mules into Washington, D.C., were reenacting Jesus' triumphal entry into Jerusalem.

Just like Jesus' donkey ride, the prophets of the Hebrew Bible would perform signs to symbolize their prophetic messages. For instance, Jeremiah broke an earthenware jug to illustrate the coming judgment (Jeremiah 19); buried rotten soiled cloth to symbolize the moral condition of his society (Jeremiah 13); to illustrate the point that Israel would be taken into bondage, he walked around with a yoke on his shoulders (Jeremiah 27–28); Isaiah warned of the invasion of Assyria by walking naked through the streets of Jerusaelm (Isaiah 20).

Michael Birkel points out that Quaker abolitionist John Woolman did his own prophetic acts of what I am calling "reenactment": "He wore undyed clothing to point out the impurity of his generation, both physical and moral, since indigo used for dyes was a product of the slave trade. [He] refused to eat and drink from silver vessels, since silver was likewise a slave product. He abstained from rum and sugar because these were also the produce of slave labor. These actions were inspired by the example of prophetic symbolic behavior."

Each of these four tactics are strategies to help you think about how to read the Bible with imagination and empathy. They are intended to help us move into the text in new and different ways. Each of these have been used in different ways throughout this book to help me in my own re-reading of the book of Revelation.

Chapter 2
From Bafflement to Wonder (Revelation 1)

"The spirit is most active at the edge of our awareness."
—Jason Minnix

A number of years ago, I went on a retreat that was led by the Quaker author Parker Palmer. It was a fantastic experience, but there was one part in particular that has stuck with me ever since, and it not only led to my reading the book of Revelation differently, but also led to the writing of this book. Palmer mentioned that he never writes books about things he knows; he only writes on things that baffle him.

You know the difference, don't you?

You never Google the stuff you are sure you know; it's only the stuff where there is a little bit of a question or uncertainty that prompts you to type in your search terms. But Palmer means more than just something you have a question about: I think Palmer meant that those things that come easy for you, the things that you could do in your sleep, are often the things that have little life in them. The easy stuff doesn't really energize us in the same way that something that really challenges us does.

It's the difficult issues that wake you up and leave you laying in bed all night mulling them over. Those things that baffle you, those things that confuse you, that you can't quite get a grip on—there's real life in that. It might sometimes feel stressful, there might not always be clear a solution, but I have found, at least for myself, that Palmer is right. It is usually in the bafflements that I come alive.

Here are a few other synonyms for "baffle," which are all pretty great: puzzle, bewilder, mystify, bemuse, confuse, confound, disconcert, flummox, faze, stump, make someone scratch their head, "be all Greek to," floor, discombobulate.

We need things that baffle us; they can move us toward curiosity and wonder. We especially need this in our spiritual lives. Bafflement and curiosity are what first brought me to this study of the book of Revelation, and they are what drives much of my pastoral and theological work today.

For much of Christian history, the book of Revelation has been puzzling, bewildering, mystifying, flummoxing, and yes, baffling.

Friedrich Nietzsche considered Revelation to be "the most rabid outburst of vindictiveness in all recorded history." And another person has called it a "script for a horror movie."

There was no other book of the Bible that baffled me more than Revelation. Even though I have been studying the Bible academically and as a minister since 1997, a lot of what I read in there baffles me still, and for that, I love it.

As it happened, shortly after participating in that workshop with Parker Palmer, I was spending some time in discernment about what I should be preaching on in my Quaker community, about what came next for us? I asked myself, what topic or book of the Bible is the most baffling to me, what is the last thing I would want to preach on? And then wham, as soon as I asked the question I wished I hadn't. The answer and the question were born in the very same moment: the apocalypse of John, the Book of Revelation. After I consoled myself, pleaded with God that this wasn't a good idea, I knew that I needed to let my own curiosity be the entry point into the text and allow that to guide me into new, or at least different, readings from what I grew up with.

Why was I so worried about teaching Revelation? Why was there so much resistance? Because for most of my life, and much of the last 150 or so years of Western Christianity, the book of Revelation has been taught as a book about God's judgment, the end of the world, and who is and who is not going to be harshly judged. In other words, it has been used as a kind of threshing mechanism for many Christians and pastors to sort the sheep and the goats. It's been a text used to rally some against others and to demonstrate, whether knowingly or not, a God of violence and fury. It has also been used, sadly and ironically, as a text to justify mistreatment of creation. Many of us have heard Christians say, when dismissing care for the earth, "Why care about climate change, why care about recycling, or conservation when it is all going to burn anyway?" Often Revelation is used to justify these kinds of viewpoints. Revelation for many has been a book that espouses a theology of violence that is backed by a God of violence.

That is why I was worried about preaching this text. Not only because I knew the folks in my Quaker meeting knew this and have heard about—or used—Revelation in these ways, but because I wasn't altogether sure that there were possible, alternative interpretations.

The starting point is the basic assumption that the Bible is not a book to use or to extrapolate information out of but rather a book that is meant to help us listen to God and be faithful and learn from others how they have attempted to do the same in their own time, given their particular challenges. On the one hand, as my friend Bill Zuelke says, the Bible is "reflective stories, attentive noticings, and deliberative actions derived from authentic encounters with the divine." And on the other, I also believe, along with Rev. Dr. Liz Theoharis, that the Bible is "a collection of stories of poor people uniting across difference to build a social movement and winning." What is amazing is that the book of Revelation actually is a perfect joining of both of these definitions.

Revelation is a perfect test case for bafflement—what if instead of avoiding what challenges us, we met the challenge with imagination and curiosity? I think that by reflecting and listening to these texts, we will be helped in our listening to God and in our own relationship to scripture, while also learning about how to resist empire as people of faith.

"We were not the intended audience of Revelation."
-Eric Barreto

Second, we were not the intended audience of Revelation. For some, this will be the most challenging pill to swallow because many pastors have taught their congregants that, "Yes, the Bible was written long ago and far away, but every word in there is the direct word of God for you and for me." I want to suggest that this just isn't true. We need to do some background work. We need to know what it is we are reading and who it is we are reading about so that we make the proper connections and interpretations. The Bible, as with everything else, can be made to say whatever we want it to say, and in the context of religion, this is a very powerful and precarious position.

So let me say it again: the book of Revelation was not written for you and me. It's not our book. It's not addressed to us, and it is not addressed to people in our time. And if this is true, then we can also safely assume that it wasn't meant to predict our future or act as a kind of magical fortune-telling book even though it has often been treated that way in American Christianity over the last 150 years or so. It doesn't represent our world. At least not at first. We have to first recognize that this book was written for a completely different group of people, living in a completely different period of time and under radically different circumstances. And once we are able to get there, then I believe we might begin to see the connections for our world today.

We have a lot of work to do if we are to get to the bottom of what is going on in this book.

> Blessed is the one who reads aloud the words of the prophecy, and blessed are those who hear and who keep what is written in it; for the time is near. John to the seven churches that are in Asia.
>
> (Revelation 1:3–8)

This is to say that when John was imprisoned on the island of Patmos and had this divinely inspired daydream, what he wrote down was first and foremost for the churches he provided care for in Asia Minor.

The biblical text is always, first and foremost, a localized, historical work. The Bible teaches us that God always speaks directly to the people where they are at, to what they are facing, to their fears, and about their celebrations.

As Eugene Peterson writes, "Where you live, where you pray is essential to who God is and reveals himself to be."

We have too often treated Revelation as a code that is to be broken or a secret formula to solve our problems. This matches this; that matches that, and "Voila! President So and So is the anti-Christ."

We should not be tricked into this way of reading any of the Bible—as though it holds a secret or that it is detached from the people for whom it was written (cf. Luke 12:2). Faith is not a math formula. As we read through these passages, let me encourage you to avoid the Revelation-as-code approach.

And yet we have to recognize that when we read Revelation, not only we are not the intended audience for this book, but its meanings are not easy for us to get at. This requires some real humility. Westerners really like the common sense approach to reading the Bible: "I read it, and whatever makes the most basic sense, that's what it means." While this is one way to read the Bible, I'd like to suggest that it's not only a very dangerous approach (following this you get all kinds of potentially damaging ideas that run counter to a God who is love) but it is also not the way Christians have read the Bible for thousands of years. Throughout church history, the Bible has been read as a book written by a community, meant to be read within a community of interpreters—it is never up to just me to figure out its meaning. Reading the Bible takes training, understanding of history, tradition, different genres—it takes work.

One of my professors in seminary liked to talk about Revelation as a kind of political cartoon. Until we are well-acquainted with the people it was written to and the times it was written in, the joke will be lost on us. Can you imagine someone opening up an archive of Facebook posts in two thousand years and reading something you wrote yesterday without any context or previous knowledge of what our world is like today? And then, if they took those few statements and made them the rule of their lives? This might make for an interesting case study!

Of central importance in understanding the book of Revelation is knowing that a man named John wrote a letter from prison to several small communities, the members of which were minorities in their culture and who were being harassed and even killed by the powers of empire. Much to the contrary of what we have been taught, Revelation's sympathies lie with the marginalized and the persecuted within the dominant Roman empire. The original hearers of the Revelation were an oppressed people.

Daniel Berrigan writes that John of Patmos was

> in a slave camp, in exile on a rock. Because, as he said, he preached God's word, the truth Jesus revealed. What kind of preaching brings that kind of punishment? ... Was he a kook, a vaporized freak, a non sequitor in a chain of logic, a broken link? We ask the question because it seemed as though the early church was facing the same question, at least by implication...No, he suffered for

Jesus and thereupon, in a link with all who suffer for the faith, he was granted this visionary sequence. Thus a logic of suffering vision held firm, hand to hand...The seven churches evidently also deserved the vision of John, welcomed it, and believed it. Thus the vision is for the community, not for John alone.[12]

John's letter aimed to encourage an oppressed people to not give up hope in the struggle for peace through nonviolence, to not give in to the comforts that empire offers in its attempts to lull resistance movements to sleep.

Elisabeth Schüssler Fiorenza says, "Something very strange happens when this text is appropriated by readers in a comfortable, powerful, majority community: it becomes a gold mine for paranoid fantasies and for those who want to preach revenge and destruction."

In other words, we are, predominantly, a privileged class of people, and our readings of these texts are heavily influenced by this privilege, which spills out in all kinds of ways. I especially think about those of us who are white, male, cis-gendered, middle-class, educated, American, Christian—people who have been the vast majority of interpreters of these texts for far too long. White supremacy and Christian supremacy are a thing. And we have tended to read and reject the Bible based on this kind of privileged reading of the text.

This is exactly what I am talking about. The comfortable and privileged must read these texts with fear and trembling, recognizing they are not our stories. By recognizing these are not our stories, we can learn from them and be helped by them.

In other words, when I read myself into the text as a white, middle class male, I read it for those experiences that I can identify with; I read it to justify where I already am; I read it to assure me of my place in the story. So long as I read this text from a privileged perspective, I will not allow it to disrupt my notions of privilege. I will not allow it to lead me into holy bafflement. I may be content to read the text, but I will refuse to allow the text to read me. Allowing the text to read me is working to listen inside the story, rather than superimposing what I want and need out of the text.

And then of course, there are many who despise the fact that people use the Bible to justify patriarchy, racism, homophobia, transphobia, misogyny, classism—and therefore reject the Bible altogether. In this view, we see the Bible as the cause of these oppressions, when, in reality, the problem may be the privilege with which many read the Bible.

Imagine if I were watching a movie in 3D, but I was watching it with sunglasses rather than 3D glasses. I sit and watch the film, thinking that not only do I not see what's so great about 3D, but it's also hard to see. Why's it so dim? Why's the color so bad? I make up my mind to never watch another 3D film again. Then, what if to my shock, my friend shows up in the middle of the film, grabs the sunglasses off my face and replaces them with a pair of 3D glasses. The film was never the problem; it was my orientation to the film, my lens, my perspective that kept me from seeing just how powerful it really is.

As long as I think that I am the primary audience, or that my experiences, my needs, and desires are the primary focus and perspective of the text, I will be watching the movie without the right glasses. I'll miss the whole thing.

Instead, I want to suggest that the intended audience is not the privileged but the oppressed, and we must learn how to read and hear others read the text from the perspective of the oppressed, from those who are victims and survivors, from those on the margins. This is counter to how Christians in the West have typically approached the Bible, but it's the right thing to do, and when we do this, we will experience something akin to putting on 3D glasses that allow us to see the Bible dynamically for the first time. "Reading the Bible from the social location of the oppression does not call for the treatment of all biblical interpretations as equals, where the interpretation from the margins is but one competing perspective. Rather, an affirmation and an option are made for the interpretations of the disenfranchised, taking priority over the interpretations of those who still benefit from societal structures of oppression."[13]

This brings me squarely to the thesis of this whole book: I do not believe Revelation has anything to do with predicting the end times but has everything to do with how small, minoritized communities of faith survive the onslaught of empire. It gives them tools for how to survive in a world where everything around them is completely off-center and seeks to create an alternative moral imagination for those who wish to resist empire.

If we are able to reorient the way we read this text, it will not only undercut the villainizing, scapegoating, and violence that has occurred from a privileged, imperial reading of the text, but it can also be used as a text that helps us to resist empire and transform it from within.

Query

So what if we became curious about our lenses, knowing we can never fully see them, but to at least wonder why this was a source of hope for the original communities, not giving them a way out of but more deeply into and through their daily suffering, holding them together when everything was telling them to fissure and fracture.

If we allow this shift in perspective to happen, the book of Revelation can sharpen and enliven our imaginations for a better understanding of how people of faith can challenge empire today.

John begins by saying, "I was in the Spirit on the Lord's day," which to me sounds a lot like when we talk about being fully yielded to God's spirit, fully aligned within our inner and outer selves so that we are able to listen to and hear God's word for us.

Revelation reveals God's concern for his people who are crushed and marginalized by those in power. It shows who God sides with. And what it reveals will challenge the comfortable, powerful, and privileged.

It is a letter of hope and courage to a people whose way of life and understanding of God was the cause of cruelty, imprisonment, and hatred. It is a letter meant to spark the imagination of nonviolent resistance. The central image that forms the Christian imagination is the lamb that was slain, the lamb who did not fight back, who was crucified, and who God honored as the innocent victim. This is a total reversal from humanity's constant effort to project blame on to the scapegoat.

These are the words being smuggled in to small bands of Christians taking on a powerful and terrifying force.

These are the words that call readers to be in solidarity with one another, no matter how distressing the situation becomes. And to know that the time of Jesus present with us is at hand.

Eugene Peterson says this:

I do not read the Revelation to get additional information about the life of faith in Christ. I have read it all before in the law and prophet, in gospel and epistle. Everything in the Revelation can be found in the previous sixty-five books of the Bible. The Revelation adds nothing of substance to what we already know. The truth of the gospel is already complete, revealed in Christ. There is nothing new to say on the subject. But there is a new way to say it. I read the Revelation not to get more information but to revive my imagination (xii-xii). It is not a question of what does this mean, but rather how does this work in our community of believers? It is not a code to be broken but a book meant to evoke our wonder (xiii).[14]

Revelation teaches us that the remedy for bafflement is wonder. I hope that you will allow this time of reflecting on Revelation to evoke wonder in you and to help shape your imagination for the ways in which God can move and change us.

Chapter 3
Light Walking Around
(Revelation 2-3)

I remember when the Boston Marathon bombing took place. We were still living on the West Coast, but it was clear that all of America's collective attention was tilted toward the East. Every news source, every line posted to social media, and many of the prayers offered up were on behalf of those who were injured, killed and/or traumatized that fateful Monday.

Some of my friends couldn't get enough of the news. While others just wanted to get away from it. One of the things that Monday in Boston did for all of us who live in America was remind us of the simple fact that evil is all around us. We don't have to know the motives of the brothers, or whether they were helped by some terrorist network to know that these two young men were drawn into a seductive evil that is far more overwhelming than even they understood.

This evil is seductive because it can pull even the most unsuspecting people into its influence and service.

And this evil ebbs and flows. Sometimes there is a little breathing room, a moment of relative calm; sometimes it feels like everything is caving in around you.

The Boston Marathon bombing was one more reminder that in America, just as in the rest of the world, we are surrounded by evil that we don't always understand and that has seductive power to draw people into its service.

If we were in the first century we would call this evil the "Roman empire," and we would talk about those who were seduced by its ways of idolatry with imperial gods, ambivalence in faith, and participation in the empire's economy. For John's seven churches, we find that the letters are less about dealing with extreme persecution—although there is some present—and more about dealing with the seductive powers of the empire's evil.

Looking back at history, it seems like there were at least two ways to end those who resisted the empire: one was to kill any resisters, which the previous emperor Nero tried to do with those who identified as followers of Jesus of Nazareth for instance, but when that did not work, the focus seems to be—as you can see here in Revelation 2–3—more on seducing all people into participation of the religion, economics, and ideology of the empire.

If you can kill the radical heart of the Christian movement—which was not just about love but about resisting the powers that denigrated human bodies and souls, forgiveness, radical hospitality, and generosity—then you don't need to actually kill Christians. And so this does seem to be a tactic that made some progress with early Christians.

As you can guess, these tactics are still at play in our world today, and there are many ways in which people of faith can find themselves seduced by the evil of empire and drawn away from the light and life of Jesus. There are many ways that we all see this take place, but when events like the Boston Marathon bombing happen, we are given a new opportunity to gauge our hearts.

If we are seduced, we may be given to hatred—not just feeling vengeful, but actually seeking revenge. This need for revenge against a wicked other was never more clear in my mind than the days after September 11, 2001. The increase in hatred for Muslims and for Arab countries by people claiming to be Christians is clear evidence of hearts that have been seduced by empire. When the church is seduced by empire, it forgets the centrality of Jesus' teachings on love of neighbor and of enemy, the practice of forgiveness, and the reality that there is always more at work than we first understand or perceive.

If we are seduced, we may be given to ambivalence. You were neither hot nor cold. This is for those who fall asleep, even though they are awake, those who have the appearance of being alive but are dead.

And finally, fear is another way we can be seduced. Fear that we can do nothing to change the world. Fear of one another. Fear works against what Jesus has called for his disciples because he has called them out into the world to love, to make peace, and to offer mercy.

John's apocalyptic letter is written into a situation similar to the seductions of our own time, but it is far more grave. Apocalypse means an uncovering or a revealing, but it is generally reserved for times when all hope is lost. Given the geographical area and the order of the churches in Revelation 2–3, it is clear that this letter was read aloud in each church and had a circuit throughout Asia Minor (it takes about ninety minutes to read aloud). Eugene Peterson in his book *Reversed Thunder* points out that the letters from John to the seven churches in Asia Minor offer direction, affirmation, correction, and motivation. This is an imprisoned pastor's letter to small, minority faith communities, trying to resist and survive during perilous times.

Which does make me wonder what it must have been like to be *Sardis* or *Laodicea* who had nothing good said about them, and whose state was read aloud to everyone. John's letters are meant to offer some way forward for these communities in a world that was unstable, dangerous, and unpredictable.

As Howard Thurman once wrote, "Much of life involves us in actions grown out of decisions that work out their fulfillment through many months and often years. It is a simple but terrible truth that, in most fundamental decisions we make, we must act on evidence that is not quite conclusive. We must decide and act on our decision without having a complete knowledge even of the facts that are involved."

Jesus' word to each church embrace their situation—the things they struggle with, the challenges of their time—and tries to help them grapple with their having been called out into the world despite the fact that they are not in control and that things are not perfect.

As these communities lean into their own challenges and seductions, John offers guardrails for them by drawing out the areas of light and life-giving forces already at work in their midst.

You probably noticed that there is a pattern that arises in John's letters—they each begin with an image or phrase from the initial vision of Jesus in chapter 1—which suggests that there is a piece of Jesus in each community. Then, each letter gives a description of the good and the correctives in each community, offers encouragements and a motivating promise—"To the victor I will give…"

I think it is important that John focuses on the strengths already present in each community:

- To Thyatira, "I know your words, your love, faith, service and patient endurance…"
- To Ephesus, "I know your deeds, labor, endurance. I know you cannot tolerate evildoers…"
- To Smyrna, "I know your affliction and your poverty even though you are rich…"

In all but two of the letters, John opens by naming the life-giving force of that particular community, and even the two he doesn't do that for, Sardis and Laodicea, he still opens with an image drawn from Jesus in chapter 1 (suggesting again that even in their waywardness, the image of Jesus is still imprinted on the center of these communities).

The key point here is that each church must draw on the graces and the life-giving forces that it already has within it. It cannot go elsewhere, for Jesus stands among them and is present to them. If they are to resist the evil and have "patient endurance" as they are repeatedly called to, then they are to draw on that grace.

John reminds Sardis, "Remember then what you received and heard; obey it, and repent;" and Ephesus, "Remember then from what you have fallen."

By refocusing these communities on powerful images connected to the vision of Jesus in Revelation 1 and drawing out their strengths, John is able to help reorient these communities around light and life that is already present. Rather than focusing solely on weakness, John is doing the pastoral work of reframing the life of these communities around gratitude and life. John knows that even the church is heliotropic and therefore tries to defend the core of who they are rather than work out all the problems within their control, let alone all those outside their control due to the regime under which they live. This reframing can give them the courage and wherewithal to move out into the darkness.

It is as the Sufi poet Rumi once wrote:

> There's an image of God deep in your heart.
> You don't need to look in some other direction. What He can subtly bestow is limitless;
> It will help you live within the world's limits
> (The Egg of the Body).

So how do we find the courage and the decisiveness to act on evidence that is not quite conclusive, and to step out into a world of evil and suffering? I believe John is showing us that we must draw on these mutually generative, life-giving places we share together.

While it may be true that there is evil, the Gospel of John reveals a counter-story about a Light that is not overcome by evil. And in Revelation, we are told about ordinary believers in tiny, powerless communities within the Roman empire who are "lamp stands." They are not themselves the Light, but they are the bright spots, the gathering points, light walking around in the world, and a training ground for acts of love, peace, and mercy in the world.

Revelation teaches us that what promotes God's work in the world is what receives commendation. Regardless of where it comes from. This is the Light at work in the world. This is the Light that cannot be overcome.

And in the midst of evil days such as the Boston Marathon bombing, we can also Light and Life. Danielle Elizabeth Tumminio writes for CNN, "There are ordinary people who step out into danger, into darkness, to shine a light. On the day of the marathon bombings, bystanders who could have protected themselves rushed to help the injured. Doctors, nurses, and their assistants worked overtime to make sure that those affected received the care they deserved, while law enforcement officials sought justice on the city's behalf. Bostonians came out to offer marathoners juice and a bathroom, even as officials told them to stay indoors. A nearby restaurant called El Pelon Taqueria gave out free food, drinks, cell phone charger outlets, and the 9-year-old daughter of the owner, Addison Hoben, decorated to-go bags with the words, 'It's going to be alright' and 'We're not afraid.'" Revelation reminds us that while the evil will not conquer the Light, we have our own role to play in the whole thing.

One way in which I believe that Revelation can be helpful to us today is to remind us to draw on our strengths, our successes, the Light that is already at work among us and out there as well. We can step out into danger even if the evidence is inconclusive. And I believe that we will find more Light walking around along the way.

Chapter 4
The Lamb that Was Slain (Revelation 5)

Two Religions

Revelation addresses these same issues of fear, control, and violence in its portrayal of the two religions: the religion of empire and the religion of creation, or as we will refer to the latter here, the religion of the lamb that was slain. It is important here to not see religion as an inherently negative word, as it is often misunderstood today. Wes Howard-Brook defines religion by its root *religio*, which means "to bind together." Therefore, *religio* is understood as those "attitudes, beliefs, and/or practices that bind individuals together as a 'people.'" Think about it this way: what bind us together in society today? What about music? Sports? Politics? Various identities? Anything can function as a religion if it is being used to bind individuals together as a people. This is critical for understanding Howard-Brook's thoughts around the religion of empire and the religion of creation—both have ways of binding people together.

> All people are inevitably and unavoidably drawn into the fray, or at least its consequences, by the fact of sharing this beautiful, abundant, yet fragile and finite planet as our home. We can always choose to run away, to

be silent, or to hide, but we cannot choose not to participate.[15]

If this is true, then Revelation is unmasking patterns, behaviors, practices, and liturgies of the empire, and it reveals a counter-narrative—a counter religion—with its own counter narratives, practices, and liturgies. The religion of empire is a religion that biblical scholar Wes Howard-Brook defines as one that people may say is grounded in God but is a human invention. It is about "justify(ing)and legitimat(ing) attitudes and behaviors that provide blessing and abundance for some at the expense of others."

On the other hand, you have a second kind of religion, the author calls the religion of creation (and I'm calling the religion of the lamb that was slain) which is "grounded in the experience of and the ongoing relationship with Creator God...that leads to blessing and abundance of all people and all creation."

Table 1 shows the distinguishing characteristics of each of these two religions as they are described throughout the biblical text, as Wes Howard-Brook describes in his book *Come Out My People*.

One religion is based on violence, coercion, suspicion, and fear.

The other religion proclaims that Jesus, who was killed, is alive and that victory cannot be guaranteed but only discovered and experienced through courage, patient resistance, sacrificial love, and nonviolence: these are the contrasting remedies to what the empire offers (see table 1 for comparison).

Revelation unmasks these two patterns of human society at work in the world. This is one of the powerful things about the book of Revelation. It unveils empire.[16]

Features of the Two Religions From Wes Howard-Brook "Come Out My People"

Feature	Religio of Creation	Religio of Empire
Source of divine power	One God, the creator of heaven and earth	Many gods and goddesses
God's Home	Beyond and within creation and among people	In a temple near the palace in the royal city
Places of sacred encounter	All of the Earth	Urban temple, mediated by priestly elite
Basic social structure	egalitarian kinship	hierarchical patronage
Basic economics	gift, barter, collaboration amid abundance	money, debt, competition amid scarcity, capital
Political ideology	God alone reigns	Human king reigns as presence of supreme god
Religious obligations	Love and praise of God and neighbor	Rituals expressing loyalty to "patron" human or divine
Relationship with 'strangers'	Hospitality, love	Suspicion, scapegoat, violence
Relationship with Land	Belongs to God, people are tenant	Belongs to king and those who can afford to buy it
Relationship with 'enemies'	Love them	Destroy the them

Table 1

Stranger / Enemy Relationships	Violence of the empire meant to control those who oppose its regime and ideologies	The church is to be shaped by the image of the lamb, a powerful symbol of nonviolence
Economics	Benefit some at the expense of the many. Mark of the Beast	The economics of the lamb call for the abundance of gift economics, care for the poor, a complete refusal to participate of imperial economics (the mark) which is symbolized in chapter 18 by slavery of both cattle as well as human bodies.
	Constant remarks about the rich, pitfalls of wealth, and deep critique of economic system in Chapter 18	
Worship / Liturgy	For every scene of heavenly worship we find a competing worship from the empire. We know that Rome had many temples and its own religious system in place. The religion of empire even has it's own competing liturgy and symbols of worship to form its subjects into its own likeness.	The lamb has his own Liturgy, which is symbolized by the suffering prophetic servant of the lamb at its center worship. This worship is slow and intentional, couched in between silence, taking on lengthy periods of hymns that lift up and center the victims of empire and those who "will shed no more tears."
Creation of a Social order	Builds a society with a center and margins, with a hierarchy and patriarchalism built in. (scapegoating sameness / multitude - difference)	Builds a community that refuses scapegoating, is rooted in unity around difference, builds the what the book of Revelation calls "the multitude."

Table 2

The first pattern is what I am calling the religion of empire because it is a whole system of making meaning and creating systems of oppression. This is akin to what the Apostle Paul calls "the powers and principalities." The religion of empire is signified by the Beast, a powerful, destructive force that seeks to destroy all that resists it. The religion of empire seeks to subject all it deems threatening. It breeds suspicion of the other and scapegoats those who get in its way.

The second pattern marks an alternative path for humanity. The religion of creation or the lamb that was slain is about direct encounter with God, building a sharing economy in which everyone has enough (rooted in texts like Exodus 16; Jesus' feeding of the five thousand; The Lord's Prayer; and the notion of Jubilee and debt forgiveness). It is rooted in a narrative where pain and suffering and those who are marginalized are incorporated into the center of community, and it seeks to build the multitude or the beloved community.

In table 2 is revealed the value system of each religion.

Then I Saw...a Lamb

Fear, desire for control, and violence are some of the main qualities that tend to show themselves when our lives feel like they are spinning out of control.

When we first learned about our oldest daughter's allergies I felt all three of these responses. I was afraid because I didn't know what it meant for our family. What changes would we have to make? What kinds of things would Lily miss out on as a kid? How might this affect her emotionally, psychologically, spiritually? What if she was accidentally given peanuts when she was out of view or away from home: could we lose our child to something like a peanut allergy?

Then as a reaction to fear—a desire for control sets in. How do we control this? How do we manage it so that we can ensure that nothing bad happens to her? Even if we know it is misguided, we want control over the situation.

Finally, violence can come into play. It is easy to lose patience and "fly off the handle" when the stress of a situation induces fear. Blaming and scapegoating are also violent responses because they demean the identity of another. Families have been ripped apart by instability and chaos: disease, the loss of a child, the stress of an unstable financial situation, serious miscommunication.

When things become rickety and unstable, our response too often is first, fear, and then an attempt to control the situation. Violence and scapegoating are natural byproducts.

In Revelation 5, John the seer finds himself having an apocalyptic vision of God seated on the throne. The question is raised, who is worthy to open the scroll of the sacred text. It dawns on John that no one on heaven or on earth is worthy to open, to handle, or to even read the sacred story of God's people.

No human hands, no special techniques, no amount of orthodox belief, right living, power, or economic status qualifies anyone to break open the scroll.

All of the ways I mentioned earlier that we try to manage just don't work on the divine. They are utterly useless here.

John also weeps, just as we all weep when we realize our own incapacity, our powerlessness.

As John is confronted with his shortcomings, he realizes that the pivot point of the universe is not us, that there are mysteries bigger than our understanding, and he is humbled by the mystery.

> Then one of the elders said to me, "Do not weep. See, the Lion of the tribe of Judah, the Root of David, has conquered, so that he can open the scroll and its seven seals."
> (Revelation 5:5)

I think when John hears these words: "Lion, David, Conquered..." he hears through his own way of hearing, with his established biases, something like: "There is to come a great mighty warrior who is stronger than any empire, and any emperor, and he will crush God's enemies."

But what John *hears* the elders saying doesn't match what he *sees with his eyes*.

> Then I saw between the throne and the four living creatures and among the elders a Lamb standing as if it had been slaughtered...
> (Revelation 5:6)

John hears the elders say there is a powerful lion, a warrior like David, but what he sees is a surprise: a slaughtered lamb.

We cannot downplay the shock John would have felt. To see a slain lamb, alive, standing by the throne of God would indeed cause holy bafflement.

John experiences personally the tension between empire and creation in this scene.

The religion of empire is rooted in fear, control, and violence. It waits for powerful heroes.

The religion of the lamb is something entirely new, and it is, I believe, the central, controlling image of the book of Revelation—the phrase "the lamb that was slain" appears twenty-eight times in the book, more than any other image. Everything else can be understood and interpreted through this filter of the lamb that was slain.[17]

The Scapegoat Mechanism

You might be wondering what is the significance of a lamb showing up so frequently within the book of Revelation?

In the times of the Old Testament, during the Jewish Day of Atonement, there was a goat offered for the people's sins. But it is important to note that the goat was never killed. New Testament Scholar Marcus Borg writes that "the sins of the people were symbolically placed upon the goat, which was then driven into the wilderness (Leviticus 16:20–22). The goat was a 'sin-bearer'—but it was not killed, not sacrificed. Indeed, to have offered up a scapegoat laden with sin as a gift to God would have been sacrilege." And to bring this into our day, scapegoating happens when a person or a group is

> singled out as the cause of the trouble and is expelled or killed by the group…Social order is restored as people are contented that they have solved the cause of their problems by removing the scapegoated individual, and the cycle begins again…scapegoating serves as a psychological relief for a group of people.[18]

So think about this for a minute.

We have a lamb that was slain, functioning as a scapegoat, who was used to calm the angry mobs we are familiar with at the end of the Gospels, and it is this scapegoat that is the central image John gives his readers to shape their religious and political imaginations in the book of Revelation.

Isn't that interesting?

Here is what I think is going on: Revelation is revealing how this scapegoat mechanism is a pattern in the world.[19] The religion of empire needs a scapegoat in order for it to function properly (or scapegoats as the case most often seems to be). Empire needs victims to create its identity and to maintain social order.

Even more powerfully, as the Gospels and the book of Revelation both reveal, the scapegoat is in fact innocent. So while there may be some psychological relief from expelling the scapegoat, the underlying conflict is left unresolved.

Doesn't this shed any light on many of today's issues?

Scapegoats are used to deflect the deeper issues that we don't want to face. And don't we use plenty of scapegoats in our world today as psychological relief?

Don't we have scapegoats in our own families? Our parents, our spouses, and our children can all function in this role.

What about at work with our bosses and co-workers?

It is easy to cast the poor, the uneducated, the undocumented, or those with different politics as the real problem.

I wonder what the relationship is between the lamb of God who was slain and refugees who are expelled from their own country?

What does the lamb of God who was slain have to say about immigrants that continue to be put in the crossfire of political discourse?

What does the scapegoating of the lamb of God have to do with the scapegoating of LGBTQ persons in North Carolina and Mississippi and across this land—in families, and churches, and yearly meetings, and in our political discourse?

And what does scapegoating have to do with racism in this country?

James Cone, in his incredibly powerful book, *The Cross and the Lynching Tree*, argues that lynching was itself the scapegoat mechanism at its most horrific in this country and reveals the very clear but often overlooked relationship between the African American experience in this country and the lamb of God who was himself lynched.

This temptation to expel others for our own psychological relief is all around us.

Just like in the 1988 film, *They Live*, where the main character played by Roddy Piper, puts on a special pair of glasses he finds and is able to see reality for what it is, Revelation is an unveiling of just how destructive the scapegoat mechanism is at work underneath the surface of our social order.

It tells us that there are two systems at work: there is one that relies on antagonisms and the expulsion of a scapegoat in order to keep the social order in balance. It is rooted in scarcity, fear, and suspicion. Wherever violence is threatened, expulsion of the victim is used to maintain the system.

But there is another way—a way of life that begins by situating this image of the lamb of God who was slain at the center of what the church understands itself to be.

This way of life is rooted in sacrificial and unconditional love. It turns strangers into neighbors and needs no victims, no scapegoats, and no enemies to exist. One that begins and ends in nonviolence—creation *ex nihilo* or "out of nothing"—understanding that all of creation is the handiwork of God.

Can you imagine what this looks like?

- John in chapter 7 of Revelation called it the Multitude.
- Martin Luther King Jr. called it the Beloved Community.
- George Fox and early Quakers called it gospel order.
- Jesus called it the Kingdom of God.

These are images of an alternative religion that calls for a community without antagonism rooted in the life and teachings of Jesus—the one who was slain, who rose, and is present among us today, draws us into this life where we truly can embody the beloved community here, where no enemy is needed to unify us.

This alternative religion is not afraid or suspicious of the world, enemies, or strangers. Instead of forcing people under labels and into hiding, the religion of the lamb is about turning strangers into neighbors and extending a hand to enemies.

The Religion of the Lamb as an Alternative

The religion of the lamb knows that it cannot force victory, and it cannot predetermine outcomes. Instead, it exercises patient endurance—a constant refrain throughout Revelation, that first century Christians are called to be patient in faithfulness rather than effective at all costs.

The power of the lamb comes not through a show of power but through lives of nonviolence and sacrificial love—that the lamb was first killed enabled him to unveil the lie that might equals right and subverts the human assumption that God is a violent God demanding the sacrifice. Instead, as James Alison notes, it is humans who demand the sacrifice; we just tend to blame it on God.

The lamb that was slain is God's revelation to humanity that God is in fact not the violent God of empire but the nonviolent God who is revealed in Jesus Christ. All of the militaristic imagery and violence of Revelation is a result of the violence of the empire that crushed and silenced much of humankind for the sake of its own survival. The lamb of God gives us an alternative vision of what the world might be.

The fact that this image is ironic and that it results in bafflement should capture our imaginations and draw us toward this second religion.

This lamb that was slain is central to shaping the first century Christian imagination: it is about patience rather than effectiveness; it is about subverting and resisting the wiles of empire, trusting that to follow the cross is about sacrifice rather than by the exploitation that is at the root of the religion of empire. If the cross is not about getting our way or taking the upper hand, then the orientation toward one another, the world, and even ourselves begins to shift. It is very hard to get to the Constantinianism, the Crusades, colonialism, and chattel slavery, when driven by these principles rooted in the lamb that was slain.

Jesus demonstrated that the cross is in fact about giving up the right to control the outcomes, to die to our own personal causes. It also reveals that society is built on mechanisms of violence, scapegoating, and exploitation. The church can either play into these systems and become comfortable, or resist them, but this resistance is both hard and costly. It is a way of learning how to lose and how to lose in just the right kind of way. Many are obsessed with being right, winning, and even dominating that, as St. Paul once said, the wisdom of the cross is foolishness to those who do not get it. This is why we usually use words like "surrender" and "sacrifice" when we talk about the cross. Through the cross, God shows us how to lose in just the right kind of way.[20]

It raises these questions:
- What would it look like for us to surrender or sacrifice in long-standing family feuds?
- What would it look like for us to give up the need to control the outcomes in our dealings at work?
- What might it look like for us to not get our own way when it comes to how we conduct ourselves as a church?
- What would it look like if the church, a denomination, or a yearly meeting, were willing to lose? Would we actually be able to let go rather than being dead-set on being right and winning?

If the cross is about practicing this kind of nonviolent love and losing in just the right kind of way, then it isn't primarily just about renouncing physical violence, but it is about creating a community where human dignity, respect, and love are the underlying principles. Parker Palmer puts it this way: "Violence is any way we have of violating the identity and integrity of another person.... [Whereas] nonviolence is a commitment to act in every situation in ways that honor the soul."

Can this blood-stained image of the lamb that was slain baffle the church enough to radically transform its imagination, radically shift its orientation toward those on the margins in ways that reflect and honor the religion of the lamb that was slain?

Closing Queries

- How do our fears and our desire for control manifest in compulsions that violate the dignity, experience, and lives of those we are in community with, those within our care, those in our family, and those with whom we interact at work, in public, and as a nation?

- How might we live, interact with, adjust our expectations for, and even ask questions of in ways that better honor others?

- How might we strengthen our commitment to being a fellowship where everyone is safe enough for their soul to show up?

- How might we live in such a way that we affirm our belief that every person has that of God within them and is worthy of honor?

Chapter 5
Finding Our New Song (Revelation 7)

The All-Day bird, the artist,
whitethroated sparrow,
striving
in hope and
good faith to make his notes
ever more precise, closer
to what he knows.
"Claritas" by Denise Levertov

Ever More Precise

I love this sentence:

> Striving in hope and good faith to make his notes ever more precise, closer to what he knows.

Isn't this beautiful? I love this image of the bird struggling to find the right notes, "closer to what he knows."

I think this image connects to something deep within all of us—it certainly does with me. One of the things I desire more than anything else is that the tune, the melody inside my head and my heart, can become the song that I sing with my life.

I want the song of my heart to be the song that is sung through my work, my play, my preaching, my caregiving, my fathering, and like this little bird, I want it to be a beautiful song.

But it isn't always easy to line up head and heart, life and song. I remember when someone I looked up to and loved told me that to become a minister was a worthless pursuit and something I would regret later in life. Sometimes those we love—those we look up to—try to keep us from singing the songs of our hearts.

Often when we try to sing our song, like this all-day bird, there are others who tell us that we can't sing, that our song is no good, that we are singing life in the wrong way.

In the previous chapter we focused on the central image of Revelation—the lamb that was slain—and about the religion of the lamb that was based on courage, patient resistance, sacrificial love, and nonviolence. We described nonviolence using Parker Palmer's definition: "Nonviolence is a commitment to act in every situation in ways that honor the soul." In other words, if this little bird is to learn its tune, if it is to make it more precise, then it needs the conditions, the support, the community in order to exercise its notes.

The world that the young Jesus movement was born into—the world that John's revelation pierces—was not a world where the conditions were perfect or safe; it was not a warm and welcoming environment for a little song bird's new song. And so John's message in Chapter 7 is that if we want to sing our new song about the lamb, then we will need to recognize that it is going to go against the grain and that we are going to need help to do it because there are those who do not want the song to be sung.

Sirens

In the previous chapter we discussed how Revelation describes two kinds of religions in conflict, the religion of empire and the religion of the lamb that was slain. Each religion has its ways of responding to strangers, enemies and neighbors alike; each shapes response to "the other."

Each of these religions also has its own liturgy, and with it comes hymns—songs of oppression or songs of liberation. The empire's song is something like the sirens in Homer's *Odyssey*. The sirens were dangerous and beautiful creatures—a cross between bird and woman—and lured nearby sailors with their enchanting music and voices to wreck on the rocky coast of their island.

This siren song sounds beautiful, but if heeded, the outcome will be disastrous. John's vision is resistance to this siren song that will stop at nothing until the whole world is left wrecked. John tells his readers that the empire's siren song, its hymnal for worship, sounds like four horses:

It is like a white horse, wearing a bow and crown, that "conquers to conquer" by thriving on international conflict and war.

It is like the red horse, bearing a great sword that breeds civil war and other conflict within its own people based on suspicion, estrangement, and alienation.

It is like the black horse, carrying a pair of scales that represents an economic system that not only strips the earth of its resources but that is based on exploitation of the poor.

And it is like a pale green horse that is accompanied by death. It aims to be the song that lulls humanity into the lie that death and violence and fear are the final word for this life. That our imaginations, our hearts, our very lives should be limited by death.[21]

The empire will stop at nothing to usurp God's song. If it has its way, it will never permit this all-day bird to sing its most faithful and honest tune.

There are singers in Revelation who sing a counter-song. In fact seven times throughout Revelation, John shows us what that looks like: worship. Revelation 5:9 calls it a new song, and you can see it is new because it is a song that Pharaoh in Egypt and Domitian in Rome do not want sung.

The New Song of the Lamb

This new song of the lamb that was slain has an entirely different tune, and not only does it subvert empire, it works to bring about a new creation under the guidance of the lamb.

This song is different and new because it is sung by imperfect voices, courageous voices, and voices that have been told not to sing.

It is a song sung by many voices, heard in the marketplaces and in the corners of empire.

It can only be heard by those who pay close attention, by those whose hearts are open, and by those whose imaginations aren't already marked by death.

Maybe those who sing this new song are a little like Odysseus's crew who first have to put beeswax in their ears so that they are not wooed by the siren song. They find ways to not only subvert but also to resist the temptations of empire by whatever means possible.

When John asks who can withstand the four horses of empire, it is this great multitude singing this new song that he sees.

This new song of the lamb is different because rather than scattering, sorting, and creating suspicion, this is a song that gathers together in "a great multitude of people that no one can count from every nation, from all tribes and peoples and languages standing before the lamb" (7:9).

This is a song that expands and includes. This is a song that invites you to lift up your voice and sing and to let this song become the song of your heart so that it is more precise, more rooted and grounded in this alternative way of the lamb.

John knows that those who sing this song will know that they are going against the grain and that they will need help. To sing this song, his parishioners in his seven little churches could get killed.

To sing the song of the lamb is to go against the grain of this world. It is to make a break with those under the siren song of empire—and as history tells us, empire sometimes includes those in the church as well as those on the outside who have succumbed to its misguided tune.

It is possible that singing this song may earn disapproval from fathers and mothers, from bosses, teachers, pastors, and from others we love. But John, at the end of chapter 7, reveals the lamb as a shepherd, guiding his people and tending to their needs.

Those who have made the break, who have learned to sing what is truly in their hearts, are the participants in a new community, singing a new song alongside the lamb of God who is their shepherd.

There will be tears in their singing, and "God will wipe those tears away," but this isn't about the warm, fuzzy wiping away of tears. These are the tears of real change from a people whose very lives, whose very reputations, whose very song is on the line.

These are the tears of creation, of the conflict and clash that results as the new invades the old. This is a comforting message to those diverse peoples living out a different vision of the world—an alternative story that is not marked by a siren song of death, but by the life giving, soul-honoring, people gathering, courageous song of new creation.

Queries

- Are we willing to shed tears for the change that is required? Are we ready and willing to sing this song and to march against the grain if that is where the lamb takes us?

- What would it take for us to learn this song as our own?

- What would it look like for us to be like the all-day bird whose precision rests on hope and good faith, development, and working the fine tuning necessary to make one's song of life truly reflect the beauty and truth that is buried within our souls?

Chapter 6
Resistance Is the Work of the People (Revelation 12)

One of the signs of a true artist is a willingness to work patiently and lovingly with even the most inferior materials.
—David James Duncan

David James Duncan's novel *The Brothers K*, is about a family that lives in Camas, Washington, the place where I pastored for six years before moving to Greensboro, North Carolina. Papa, one of the main characters in the book, is a paper-mill worker who has gone semi-professional in baseball. He does fairly well as a pitcher for his team until he has his thumb crushed in an accident at the mill.

Consequently, he falls into depression and abuses substances. In an attempt to regain ground, he builds a shed in the backyard where he begins to practice his pitching again.

After building the shed, Papa says to his son, Kade, about the shed:

> The thing is...I don't want you getting worked up over nothing when I start spending time out here. I built this shed because throwing baseballs keeps my head on straight. I did *not* build it to inaugurate some sort of fairytale comeback. . . .

No matter how well I may eventually seem to be throwing, and no matter what your all-knowing brother Everett may say, all I'm ever gonna do out here is toss the pitchers' equivalent of harelip prayers. Okay? . . .

Don't think of it as baseball, Kade. Call it my hobby, or some weird kind of worship maybe. Call it psalmball, or shed ball, or thumbball if you like. But remember it's not baseball. It's not a comeback. You've got to promise me that).

And then Papa pitches:

Papa wasn't kidding about "harelip prayers," though. His resurrected pitches were fast, event to Everett's educated eye, but shockingly wild. We soon grew accustomed to the resounding thwham! of balls denting the bare garage siding [instead of hitting their intended target, an old mattress], followed by a whump! inside the shed (Papa's fist slamming the wall)...[followed by choice words spoken] and a palpably disgusted silence. Every time he fell into one of these funks I expected to see him stalk out of the shed and into the house to announce that he'd sworn off his new hobby forever. But instead, sooner or later, out would come another scorcher, which usually also missed the mattress and blasted the bare wall so hard I half expected the ball to stick.

I love this description because the materials he uses for his hand-built shed are seemingly inferior, just like his thumb. The inferiority of the materials at his disposal are matched only by the persistence with which he goes out night after night, throwing that baseball. He didn't do this with the hope that some day he would become a pro again, but because he hoped to recover his dignity, that the muscle memory of throwing a ball would return to his once well-trained arm, and that he could create something out of those pitch-turned-prayers that might bring life back to him.

I'd like to suggest to you that the building of this shed and the persistent practice of throwing those wild pitches was for Papa a kind of liturgy. He took what earthly, vulnerable materials he had, and he turned them into beautiful art that was less about what he knew and more about what he had worked to create.

Too often those within the church believe that liturgy or ritual is empty and meaningless, but Papa shows us the reverse. There is nothing dead about Papa's pitching because what he is creating, one pitch at a time, is a new story.

Two Liturgies

In Revelation 12 we see not one but two kinds of liturgy at work. It falls right in the middle of three scenes of worship that take place between chapters 11 and 15—with a dramatic conflict symbolized by a dragon and a woman, Michael and angels, and then two beasts in chapter 13. John is showing that the two religions both have their own respective liturgies.

> In *Unveiling Empire,* Wes Howard-Brook writes
>> This war took the form of ritual crucifixions, arena contests with lions, and other public spectacles of execution. John's insight is that these are not merely "political"

acts, but liturgical acts as well.... Even "the courtrooms with the robed magistrates, the choreographed rising and sittings, collective responses and other ritual acts" are all a part of this "liturgical demeanor."[22]

In other words, the empire's religion of temples, statutes, decrees, ordinances, and symbols are, for John, a kind of liturgy that dulls the hearts and minds of its subjects.

We can define liturgy as a practice that is meant to form the worshipping community in a particular way. Or as Quaker scholar Ben Pink Dandelion describes it in his book, *Liturgies of Quakerism*, liturgy is the work of the people. It is something that is done, acted, or performed by a community.

Therefore, liturgy can be used for positive or negative formation. It can be used to dull hearts, stunt imaginations, and make people content with the way things are. Worse, it can lead them to believe that the way things are is divinely ordained. (Usually it is the people on top who are most likely to believe in this unquestioned divine ordering.)

John's Revelation is written to a second-generation church, struggling with compromise and apathy. The church has plateaued. It's lost steam and direction. I believe Revelation is a letter meant to spark imaginations, reshape liturgy, inspire hope, and like Papa in *The Brothers K*, help them find life again before it is too late.

So John, couching these conflicts of the great red dragon and the pregnant woman within the context of worship, tells us something very important: Christian worship is a counter-political act.

If the liturgy of the empire is formed by public spectacles of execution, then the liturgy of the lamb is the exact opposite—public spectacles of life, care-giving, and transformation.

When I say worship is a political act, I don't mean that worship is about politics in the way we often think about politics today. Worship is not about having a platform to espouse certain ideals. I know there are plenty of churches and preachers in the news on a daily basis who use their pulpit to push certain political agendas—this isn't what I mean.

However, worship is not neutral either. What the church does in worship has an impact on how it lives in and interacts with the world. I believe that John is arguing the following:

- Worship is political in that the very act of a group of people gathering together to tell thousand-year-old stories about goodness and evil, peace and war, God and wickedness, is a practice meant to shape hearts, minds, and moral actions.

- Worship is political in as much as proclaiming the lamb that was slain and is the victor and the one true God, over every other idol and power in society, is a claim that not only shapes allegiances but is about survival for those living under oppression.

- Worship is political because it unveils the illusions of the empire. It shows the exploitation and the spectacles of death that it manifests for what they are.

- Worship is political in that it seeks to build a movement that brings about the kind of world that God intended, heaven on earth, or as we will see in later chapters, the new Jerusalem coming down out of heaven at the end of Revelation.

John's Revelation tells us something very important: Christian worship is meant to be a counter-narrative to the liturgy of empire.

Think about today's political landscape, the infighting, the victim-blaming, the attack ads, the scapegoating. This is the liturgy of empire made manifest before our very eyes. It thrives off the build-up to a sacrifice, so as to create a public spectacle of execution.

Our worship is meant to form us into living in ways that are meant to be public spectacles of life and caregiving.

I like how one theologian describes what a counter-narrative to imperial worship looks like:

> When people tell me they find Mass boring, I want to say to them: it's supposed to be boring, or at least seriously underwhelming. It's a long-term education in becoming un-excited, since only that will enable us to dwell in a quiet bliss which doesn't abstract from our present or our surroundings or our neighbour, but which increases our attention, our presence and our appreciation for what is around us. The build-up to a sacrifice is exciting, the dwelling in gratitude that the sacrifice has already happened, and that we've been forgiven for and through it [and therefore have no more need of sacrifice or scapegoats] is, in terms of excitement, a long, drawn-out let-down.[23]

What I like about the liturgy of Papa's baseball shed and his psalmball is that instead of abstracting himself from the pain of his situation, he enters into this long and drawn out process of squaring with that pain and being transformed by it.

His liturgy is one in which brokenness, weakness, and his inferior thumb is not something to be gotten rid of but that actually becomes the material through which he patiently and lovingly begins to craft a new story for his life. Rather than escaping or evacuating from his pain, he is taken deeper into it, which is where healing can be found.

Worship is the place where hearts are broken open toward the poor, the strangers, the enemies of empire. It is also where healing can be discovered amidst the suffering.

This is John's message:

> Church, if you are to survive, if you are to see through the incessant demands of the empire, then you must worship, you must be formed by the liturgy of the lamb.

John knows that worship is not aimed at something that might happen someday if we are good enough. Worship is the active participation in creating that different story right now. A renewed liturgy that resists the impulses of the empire is necessary if the church is to not just survive but embody the beloved community.

In Chapter 11, worship breaks out from "loud voices" saying:

> The kingdom of the world has become the kingdom of our Lord and of his Messiah, and he will reign forever and ever.
> (Revelation 11:15)

In Chapter 12, loud voices proclaim:

> Now have come the salvation and the power and the kingdom of our God and the authority of his Messiah, for the accuser of our comrades has been thrown down, who accuses them day and night before our God. But they have conquered him by the blood of the Lamb and by the word of their testimony, for they did not cling to life even in the face of death.
>
> (Revelation 12:10–11)

All of this is active. It is happening in the present moment. John is showing the seven churches in Asia Minor that they can conquer through the nonviolence of the lamb and the witness of their lives in the world. Those are the tools, the weapons so to speak. And they find their origin in the Christian liturgy of the lamb that was slain.

When we worship, something happens because when we worship we are creating something entirely new—we are, in fact, the woman who symbolizes the church, giving birth to the Christ-child in the world.

What Are We Creating?

So what are we creating with our individual and collective lives as the church? What are we creating when we worship together? How are we allowing our liturgies to be the shed where we practice over and over again in the hopes of forming our lives in a particular direction?

- There is a world out there, in fact just down the street, of people living in destitute poverty.
- There is a world out there struck by fear, caught in cycles of violence, exploited by an economic

system that benefits some at the expense of others.

- There is a world out there of people who are hurt and in need of healing, care-giving, and of dignity.
- There are people who deeply long to hear the new song of the lamb sung to them and to be asked to join in the chorus.
- There are people who have not yet experienced the power and the freedom that comes when we gather in silence and follow Jesus as teacher and friend.

Our concern and care for the least of these, for those who want to come and be at this table, who are in need of a community, who conquer by the lamb that was slain. The word of their testimony is our liturgy, it is our political act, it is our artistic creation—even if we feel that we are sometimes starting with inferior materials.

I want to close this chapter with a quote from Howard Thurman:

> The simplest definition of art is that it is the activity by which people realize their ideals.... We are all artists in the sense that we are all engaged in some kind of activity by which we are realizing our ideals. What kind of ideas are you realizing? There is no neutrality here. Everybody is engaged in this activity. Is what you are realizing worthy of you, or are you engaged in the realization of ideals of which you are ashamed, and before which you stand condemned in your own sight? Long, long ago, it was said by a very wise and

understanding friend, "By their fruits ye shall know them."[24]

When we come together. When we actively participate and receive the formation that comes from being shaped by the liturgy of the lamb. When we read these stories from scripture. When we live out the word of our testimony by practicing hospitality, peacemaking, simple living, truthfulness, and by proclaiming the dignity of every human being—we realize the ideals that Revelation calls us to.

Queries

- Is our practice of worship one that draws people into this work of presence and attention to what is right in front of us, or does it ultimately abstract us from the needs of our community?

- Is our liturgy of worship one where human lives are disposable, or does it take the good and the inferior materials of our lives, and not only accept them but allow the life and light of Jesus to patiently and lovingly bring about new creation?

- Does our liturgy of worship aim to exclude and scapegoat, or does it work to build up the beloved community, embracing the Kingdom of God among us?

Chapter 7
The Multitude
(Revelation 7)

I remember in 2016, I was very much surprised to find myself engrossed in party politics in the run-up to the election. I followed the news, listened to the speeches, paid close attention to the protests and the scandals.

I followed closely twitter hashtags like
#DemsinPhilly
#RNCinCLE
#BernieOrBust

If you happened to watch the conventions you'll remember that the various speakers tried to explain away or explain causes of things such as continued gun violence in this country, ongoing terrorist attacks, poverty, sexism, xenophobia, racism, and the need for marriage equality.

- In order to deal with the gun violence, we need to be very clear about who are the good people and who are the bad people.
- In order to protect ourselves from the wicked, we need more guns.
- In order to keep families strong, we must maintain narrow boundaries around what constitutes family.
- In order to be a great country, we must refuse entry to anyone who is not white.

Words likes "good and bad," "protection," "boundaries," "refuse entry," "safety," are key words in the conversation around exclusion.

There are so many examples of exclusion that take place in the United States. It happens wherever fear and discrimination adversely target people and communities with less power: redlining; white flight; discriminatory hiring practices; voter suppression; the carceral state.

What do we make of all of this?

Exclusion comes from the religion of empire's penchant for suspicion, fear, and the policing of categories.

Revealing the Empire's Social Order

Revelation reveals that the religion of empire thrives on separation. It believes some people are superior, and in order to remain superior, those who are subject must know and keep their place.

In direct opposition to this is the religion of creation, or as we are calling it, the religion of the lamb that was slain, due both to its centrality to Revelation but also because of what it stands for—nonviolence, sacrificial love, bringing all people and nations together.

As first-century Christians sought to survive and subvert empire, they were given this powerful image of the the lamb that was slain, what Quaker Bayard Rustin would reference later when he called for "angelic troublemakers":

> We need in every community a group of angelic troublemakers. Our power is in our ability to make things unworkable. The only weapon we have is our bodies, and we need to tuck them in places so wheels don't turn!

This image—the innocent lamb slaughtered as a victim of imperial violence—stands as the primary Christian example of an angelic troublemaker and is meant to shape the first-century Christian subversive imagination. This lamb becomes the center of the church's liturgy and imagination and offers an alternative to the fear, scapegoating, and sorting of empire.

In Revelation 7:9–12, surrounding this lamb is another powerful image: the multitude. Here we are given a community in contrast to the religion of empire's creation and maintenance of social hierarchies as well as its persistent use of violence by scapegoating:

> 9 After this I looked, and there was a great **multitude** that no one could count, from every nation, from all tribes and peoples and languages, standing before the throne and before the Lamb, robed in white, with palm branches in their hands. 10 They cried out in a loud voice, saying, "Salvation belongs to our God who is seated on the throne, and to the Lamb!" 11 And all the angels stood around the throne and around the elders and the four living creatures, and they fell on their faces before the throne and worshiped God, 12 singing, "Amen! Blessing and glory and wisdom and thanksgiving and honor and power and might be to our God forever and ever! Amen."

The multitude is a beautiful tapestry woven together of all of humanity, with the oppressed and minoritized at the center with the lamb.

> 13 Then one of the elders addressed me, saying, "Who are these, robed in white,

and where have they come from?" 14 I said to him, "Sir, you are the one that knows." Then he said to me, "These are they who have come out of the great ordeal; they have washed their robes and made them white in the blood of the Lamb. 15 For this reason they are before the throne of God, and worship him day and night within his temple, and the one who is seated on the throne will shelter them. 16 They will hunger no more, and thirst no more; the sun will not strike them, nor any scorching heat; 17 for the Lamb at the center of the throne will be their shepherd, and he will guide them to springs of the water of life, and God will wipe away every tear from their eyes."

Here we have a first-century version of the beloved community, a picture of radical hospitality where the victims are actually centered in their communities, and diversity of nationality, language, tribe, and people is seen as a gift..

The multitude refuses to be a quilt made up of the same color, pattern, and fabric.

The multitude finds its power and vitality in its difference. They reject the idea that unity requires sameness. Instead of purity, they choose remix (see chapter 9).

The multitude bears palm branches of peace. They refuse the tools, language, and symbols of empire and scapegoating.

The multitude learns how to hold tension and multitruth. They choose to be committed to the light of God in all people.

The multitude is able to confess when it has benefited from and been complicit with empire.

The multitude knows that we are not whole without one another. We do not have community, in the way that God envisions community, unless it is like this image of the multitude.

As Reverend William J. Barber II once said: "'We' is the most important word in the social justice vocabulary. The issue is not what we can't do, but what we CAN do when we stand together. With an upsurge in racism/hate crimes, criminalization of young black males, insensitivity to the poor, educational genocide, and the moral/economic cost of a war, we must STAND together now like never before."

We generally like this kind of community. We say we want it, but we struggle for so many reasons, not least of which is that we are swimming in a culture steeped in the religion of empire.

My hope is that the image of the multitude is something you will explore further as an image that might inspire you and your faith community as you resist sorting. As Reverend Barber said, "We must stand together now like never before." We must refuse to be sorted, and we must refuse to sort. Let us work together to create the multitude so that we might truly experience beloved community.

I want to close with this story I heard about Vincent Harding from the American Friends Service Committee. In 2013, he spoke to a room full of Quakers. His words speak to the challenge of all of us living into John's dream of the multitude.[25]

> I have been personally moved over the years by a statement of a poet who was being

interviewed on the radio back in the 1960s. As many of you know that was a period of great ferment in this country, but also in many other parts of the world including Africa. This man was from West Africa. What he said I always keep within my heart: "I'm a citizen of a country that does not yet exist."

I take that as a challenge, and I share it with my friends struggling with immigration. I tell them, "Don't fight yourself into a country that does exist, but struggle into a country that does not yet exist." America is waiting to be born.

Can you imagine that those called founders of our country, those slaveholders and slave owners, were really talking about building a democracy? But we do imagine that's what they intended. And every generation has to carry on the work that those so called founders couldn't do.

You know something about building a Quaker community, you can see it. The vision that you have is not meant to be kept to yourself, it's meant to be expressed, to trouble some people, to push some people, to embrace some people, but for you to keep saying, "I see a Quaker community that does not yet exist and I am absolutely committed to its coming into being."

The easiest way is to say, because it doesn't exist, "I am getting out of here." People will come around and rub your head and say, "What's wrong?" What you are doing is opening the breath of God and offering to others to see the Quaker community that does not yet exist. What is considered in one generation becomes possible because of the seers.

We need you to keep seeing, brother, and stay as sane as you can. Find as many accompanying insane Quaker folks to walk with you on this one, find all kinds of allies. Once you keep holding on to your vision, it will rise up out of the darkness and we will begin to know what that word Light that we use so much really means. We need you.

Chapter 8
Economics, Poverty, and Crashing the Beast's Party (Revelation 13, 18)

If there is one aspect of Revelation that has been overused and abused, and that has fallen prey to our constant temptation to make John's first century letter a document that predicts the future, it has to be the mark of the beast. What was the mark of the beast? What does 666 stand for? There are many questions when we read passages like this.[26]

What are some of the things you have heard the mark of beast represented as?

Mikhail Gorbachev's birthmark, Obamacare, enforced Sunday worship, one-world government, the United Nations, a specific year, Verichip, credit cards, taking prayer out of schools.

There are so many!

It raises a level of fascination that can be fun (or terrifying) to imagine, but there is a problem with trying to figure out the mark: we don't know the story behind the story. And when we don't know the story behind the story, we begin to read our own prejudices and assumptions into the text; this can skew our reading and understanding of Scripture. So it is essential that when we read, we remember that there is something else going on in the background that we cannot see.

There are at least two problems with trying to identify the mark, or as it is in the Greek, *eikon* (from where we derive icon), of the beast:

First, John doesn't describe it at all—so it was something that was most likely obvious to the people for whom this book was written. Second, if we read this with a future lens—as something meant to predict the future—then we begin trying to find things that correlate, which, unfortunately, leads us down a rabbit hole of totally missing the point. But if we read it as a letter meant for a particular community about surviving and subverting empire in their time, the emphasis changes dramatically.

Unfortunately, we have, no doubt, missed the point. We have been led to think that we are to always be on the lookout for some microchip, some barcode, somebody's birthmark, so that when we find it we will know what to do and what not to do. Finally, once we have the mark, everything will be made clear because we will know who is bad and who is not—who is an enemy of God and who is on the side of the lamb.

We have already seen two of the main sins of empire that John unmasks: the violence of empire that contrasts with the lamb that was slain, and the seduction of its liturgy and imperial religion, which was like a siren song and meant to form people to be its subjects. This leads us to a third sin of empire, the *eikon* of the beast, which is the empire's abusive economic practices (See especially Revelation 18).

In other words, John reveals an economic system that succeeds by creating poles within society, small and great, rich and poor, free and slave, and that is based on some living in poverty and under subjugation for the benefit of others. Wes Howard-Brook defines the religion of empire: "While sometimes claiming to be ground in that same God (as the Religion of creation), is actually a human invention that is used to justify and legitimate attitudes and behaviors that provide abundance and blessing for some at the expense of others."

Here's the critical point: deep systemic poverty is a sign that the religion of empire's beastly economic system or structure is actually doing what it is supposed to do.

Understanding Poverty

When I was in New York City a few years ago for a series of classes and forums on "The Bible as a Response to Empire" at Union Theological Seminary, one of the things that we talked about is the way that we understand poverty. There are at least four ways in which we as Americans categorize people who become poor, and our understanding of how people become poor influences how we respond to them (these ideas were presented by Dr. Colleen Wessel-McCoy):

Poverty as accident—When we see poverty as a part of economic cycles, disasters, politics, geography, racism. It is poverty as accident, which assumes that the system is generally good, but sometimes bad things happen. Responses we see to this kind of poverty: short-term assistance, plug the holes, fill in the gaps.

Poverty as pathological—When we see poverty as characterized by bad choices or (bad) certain values that create poverty. You'll hear words like "culture of poverty," used to describe this model. Responses we see to this kind of poverty: stigmatize poverty, so the poor won't want to make bad choices. If it really is that undesirable, people will just not be poor. One of the clearest examples of this was the harmful phrase "welfare queen" that got its start in the 1970s.

Poverty as fate—Poverty is inescapable and therefore it is something I must accept; some people are just going to be poor. This view can be taken from a misunderstanding of Jesus' phrase, "The poor will be with you always," or it is seen as everything happening for a reason." The response sounds something like this: Accept one's lot in life, suck it up, and go about with what you're doing. "Stop complaining, at least you have a job."

Poverty as structural—In this understanding, poverty and exploitation are not an accident, but actually the response of the out-workings of the system—the system is controlled and set up to benefit a certain, very small subset of society, while everyone else accepts their role and follows orders. Poverty is a sign, not of the system being broken, but of the system actually working the way it has been set up to work. Response to this: empower the poor to make the changes deemed necessary.[27]

Many Christians throughout history shared this fourth perspective, including Martin Luther King Jr.: "What good does it do to be able to eat at a lunch counter if you can't buy a hamburger?" He understood that we can pay lip service to rights while blocking equality in other spheres of our society.

From this perspective, it's not good enough to have a safety net or simply to plug holes. Instead, we need to ask why there are holes to begin with; what is the safety net actually covering up? It's not good enough to help pull people out of a river. We need to go upstream and find out who's throwing them in to begin with.

Unveiling the *Eikon* of the Beast

This is, I believe, what John is trying to unveil for his readers. Inequity is not about accident, pathology, or fate—it is a demonic spirit at work within the structures of the society that created it. It is the result of the spirit of empire.

John of Patmos is explaining to the seven churches that poverty is structural.

There is a certain kind of beastly economics that has been at work in the world for a very long time—if you don't play by its rules, you will not be able to buy or sell, and it may get you killed—just as in Revelation 13.

Biblical scholar Elisabeth Schüssler Fiorenza writes, "Revelation consistently speaks of the power of Satan in national, political and cosmic terms. (13, 18 20). Satan deceives the nations and not merely individuals into sinful action (20:7–8). Revelation's notion of ultimate evil is best understood today as systemic evil and structural sin."[28]

Let's unpack this a little. Revelation 13 talks a lot about the image or *eikon* of the beast. This is significant because it stands in contrast to the image of God, which we see referred to at the beginning of creation (See Genesis 1).

We can describe God's creation of the world as structuring/ordering the world to work in a certain way that are largely based on taking care of the land, animals, the sea, and one another.[29] We know from Old Testament texts like Exodus 16 and Leviticus 25 that God instructed people to take only what they need so that there would be enough daily bread for everyone, and that they were called to practice something called jubilee, where every forty-nine years everyone's debts would be canceled, and indentured servants would be freed. As a part of jubilee, they were to let the land lie fallow every seven years. Jesus, who is understood by the New Testament writers to be the completion of this creation, shows humanity how to live this out in human relationships (through radical hospitality, extending welcome to the stranger, building a movement made up of people on the margins, forgiving people for sins that kept them ostracized socially, feeding the hungry).

But in Revelation 13, we see that the beast is involved in a counter-creation story. Listen to some of the wording:

- makes the earth and its inhabitants worship the first beast
- it performs great signs
- it deceives the inhabitants of the earth, telling them to make an image for the beast
- and it was allowed to give breath to the image of the beast
- and those who would not worship the beast would kill (cf. Daniel 3:19)

So in this first portion of our text, you get this sense of the beast as a counter-creation story, breathing life into the image of the beast (cf. Gen 1:26–27), a new god that emerges out of the ground—made by human hands—and has its own structuring/ordering of things.

As Crystal Hall points out, what is going on between these two contrasting *eikons* is that Revelation shows us that the beast seeks to recreate its followers in its own image,[30] to encompass and enslave all of humankind to its own greedy and violent ends. This is exactly what we have been calling the religion of empire.

Then chapter 13 says:

16 Also it causes all, both small and great, both rich and poor, both free and slave, to be marked [be given] on the right hand or the forehead, 17 so that no one can buy or sell who does not have the mark, that is, the name of the beast or the number of its name.

Here the *eikon* of the beast symbolizes participation in the empire's economy. In fact, the Greek word for "mark" (*charagma*) means to stamp or make an impression on something. It is used when referring to imperial coins, which would have had the emperor's face marked on the coin. It is also an official seal for business contracts and the branding impressed upon prisoners, slaves, and religious devotees of the imperial religion.

This *eikon* was important to form and shape its subjects, as Wes Howard-Brook points out:

> The charagma [mark] of ancient Rome was not some esoteric symbol but a stamp used to certify deeds of sale, and the impress of the emperor's head on the coinage. The imperial currency bore the image, name, year, and titles of the emperor. This made coinage an important means by which Roman myth was propagated. These coins were an affront to those who resisted empire. As far as Revelation is concerned it was not possible to denounce Rome as satanic and simultaneously use the empire's medium of exchange—its currency (*Unveiling Empire*, 175).[31]

In writing about the image of the beast, John is attempting to unmask the true spirit behind the myth and structure of the empire—which would have told its people all kinds of things in order to keep them pacified.

Revelation is about crashing the beast's party of luxury and idolatry. John is a prophet, calling his people to come out of empire.

Come Out of Empire?

So what does it mean to come out from and resist this *eikon* of the beast?

Following Revelation, it means to be non-participants in a system that is opposed to the image of God in creation and the lamb that was slain.

But honestly, for us today this is a much harder question—especially when we see the effects of this same kind of system being built up and protected by business and government.

There is no wonder then that Christians have been tempted to find alternative readings softening John's critique or diverting it altogether. I would much rather be let off the hook here then consider how I myself may be subject to a system that uses and abuses. Or how I have helped to support that system.

Ironically, interpreting the mark as an implanted computer chip (as some do) lets us off the hook by distracting contemporary readers from what the original author intended. We should be suspect of any reading of the text that doesn't place hard questions on us.

John tells the churches all about the imperial economic system. The members of these faith communities were small in number and poor by the empire's standards. John intended, not that they might be crushed with defeat, but that they might have no illusions about what they're up against, so that they will see these structures for what they are—affronts to the way of the lamb that was slain and completely contradictory to the kind of world that God is building.

Crystal Hall helped me make the connection of this reading to what is known as the "cargo list" in Revelation 18. The whole passage is worth your time, but here is a key excerpt:

> 9 And the kings of the earth, who committed fornication and lived in luxury with her, will weep and wail over her when they see the smoke of her burning; 10 they will stand far off, in fear of her torment, and say,
>> "Alas, alas, the great city,
>> Babylon, the mighty city!
>> For in one hour your judgment has come."
>
> 11 And the merchants of the earth weep and mourn for her, since no one buys their cargo any more, 12 cargo of gold, silver, jewels and pearls, fine linen, purple, silk and scarlet, all kinds of scented wood, all articles of ivory, all articles of costly wood, bronze, iron, and marble, 13 cinnamon, spice, incense, myrrh, frankincense, wine, olive oil, choice flour and wheat, cattle and sheep, horses and chariots, slaves—and human lives.

Revelation 18 is to be read in light of Revelation 13 and John's critique of imperial economics, the critique against the empire's trade in all of these items that symbolize wealth and prestige, including the very lives of humans. John's point must not be missed here. The empire of Rome is trading in human bodies, and God damns such a practice.

15 The merchants of these wares, who gained wealth from her, will stand far off, in fear of her torment, weeping and mourning aloud,

> 16 "Alas, alas, the great city,
> clothed in fine linen,
> in purple and scarlet,
> adorned with gold,
> with jewels, and with pearls!

17 For in one hour all this wealth has been laid waste!"

This is a scathing critique of imperial economics and its reliance upon and practice of slavery. How could it be that people reading this text and being shaped by its imagination could in centuries that follow not only allow for but participate in such practices?

Our role as people of faith is to see through these illusions as well, to ask the penetrating questions, and to live as best as we can as a community grounded in the *eikon* of the lamb where there are "multitudes of every nation, from all tribes and peoples, and languages..."

Instead of perpetuating inequity, or settling for plugging its holes, we are called to bring an end to poverty altogether and never for a second participate in any economic practices that go against the principles of God's love. I believe that Revelation calls us to challenge the systems that create inequity, hungry children, houseless people, work that dehumanizes, and divisions between rich and poor, slave and free.

A few years ago there was a struggle that involved Hilton housekeepers in Vancouver, Washington, near where we lived. The full-time workers there were earning less than poverty-level wages. People were bringing in food boxes to give to the workers because they couldn't afford groceries—all of this while employed by a multi-million dollar, international corporation. They were being asked to clean more rooms for less pay, without mops or other basic tools needed to do the job efficiently or effectively. Many of these women were supporting their families; some were immigrants, some lived in Section 8 housing. They had limited rights and limited resources. Many worked multiple jobs while still having to get groceries from food banks in order to feed their families while relying on government assistance for other basics. But as they grew increasingly frustrated, finding courage in their own voices, they began to challenge this system and ask hard questions. They were, after a year-long battle, able to get a little more pay, some basic equipment, and a cap on how many rooms they were expected to clean. But this is just one example. There is plenty more work to do; this battle continues in many places and in many forms throughout the world.

The *eikon* of the beast is still at work in our world today. It just doesn't look like a barcode, and it won't be showing up as a pill anytime soon. It's been here for a long time, and it goes by many names.

Chapter 9
Revelation Is Remix
(Revelation 21–22)

I am a huge Bob Dylan fan. One of my favorite Dylan albums is titled *Self-Portrait*. The cover image is one that Dylan himself painted. In my research, I couldn't find any mention of the cover referencing anything directly, but it has a certain resemblance to Pablo Picasso's own painting, also titled *Self-Portrait*. When you line up these two images side by side you can see that there is a borrowing and adaptation from the one painting to the other. This is something that Dylan loves to do; he calls it *love and theft*. Building on, borrowing, adapting the things you love; drawing them inside, internalizing, and making them your own.

There is a second way that Dylan adapts and builds upon the works of others to make up this self-portrait album. Because it's mostly just a collection of other people's songs!

Of the twenty-three songs on the album, I count seven that Dylan wrote himself. Another five of the songs are traditional folk songs handed down by the folk community, and the rest are cover songs, put into Dylan's folk-rock style, from artists like Gordon Lightfoot, Cecil A. Null, and Paul Simon.

This self-portrait is actually a composite of other singers, songs, styles, and traditions that have presumably influenced or inspired Dylan, redone in his own style. There is truth in this: we are woven from so many different threads.

But this idea of various threads that are brought together in a way that creates something new happens in every kind of music, literature, and visual art. Creators draw on ideas, images, sounds, and styles of others in order to tell their own stories. The title of one of Austin Kleon's *Still Like an Artist* says it all.

Today we call this *remix*. Remix is to combine or edit existing material in a way that creates something new.

Now you may have heard the word *remix* from DJ culture, which is where the word originates, but the practice extends much further back in history. Today it has taken on a more popular usage to describe videos on YouTube, music of all kinds, novels, and it even describes a culture where people take music, video, books, and build with well-known beats, lyrics, or stories to create something new.

A few examples:
- Hip-Hop music using "samples" from Soul and R&B singers
- *Pride and Prejudice and Zombies* (Seth Grahame-Smith).
- *Romeo and Juliet* by Baz Burhmann

The television show *Grimm* draws ideas from the old Brothers' Grimm fairy tales to make a 21st century crime fiction that takes place in Portland, Oregon.

Fashion is always being remixed—In the 1990s, when I was in high school, a lot of us were going to the thrift shop and buying up all the old polyester shirts and velour suits. I had bell-bottoms I wore regularly, but then I'd add my own style.

Remix happens all over the place because remix is about taking what is already there, whether it is people, stories, texts, art, music, images, clothing—and then building something new out of what we've found. Remix is born out of love: it is a way to pay homage to the past while internalizing it, making it your own, giving it renewed purpose. This is in contrast to say a "cover band" that uses other material and tries to keep it totally unchanged, or the alternative course of creating something new from scratch.

Someone who makes a good remix is a person who is able to enter into the story that is already there but then finds ways to make it their own. It is about starting out with the pre-existing material but then being willing to adapt it in appropriate ways to keep it fresh and relevant.[32] When we talk about authentic faith, we might be talking about good remix—the faithful are not simply a cover band, nor are they unhooked from history, tradition, and community.

In fact, remix is in the Bible. We see something like remix in Jesus' life. He tells parables that draw on well-known imagery, people, and places: Samaritans, a well-travelled road into Jericho, the life of a shepherd or of a farmer. But then Jesus tells the story in a new way; his stories each have a hidden shocker, a challenge that works on its hearers.

People were used to hearing stories one way; Jesus flips the pattern—as we see in the Samaritan hero in the parable of the Good Samaritan. Most people were used to hearing stories about how the powerful win, or that

God will smite you if you're a wrong doer. Jesus flips these patterns. He remixes them, creating new stories (and new kinds of heroes). When Jesus said, "You have heard it said, but I say to you…" that's remix. He was so good at this kind of spiritual technology—telling spiritually subversive, remixed stories—that these parables remain with us today. The point of the remix in this case was to subvert the religion of empire and teach about God as a God of love, forgiveness, and reconciliation.

Can you guess what I'm building toward—Revelation is all remix. Just like Bob Dylan's self-portrait album, Revelation is made up of all kinds of little threads, histories, stories, images that flow together into a new picture. It builds on pre-existing material, images, and stories to give us a new picture of who God is and who we are to be as the people of God.

Consider Revelation 21–22:5. This passage is bursting with biblical remix:

- Then I saw a new heaven and a new earth… // "For I am about to create new heavens and a new earth…" (Isaiah 65:17)

- And the sea was no more (represents in ancient times a turbulent force and unrest) // "The voice of the LORD is over the waters; the God of glory thunders, the LORD, over mighty waters." (Psalms 29:3)

- And I saw the holy city, the new Jerusalem… // A thread that shows up again and again in the Hebrew Bible.

- He will dwell with them; they will be his peoples, and God himself will be with them; he will wipe away every tear from their eyes… // "My dwelling place shall be with them; and I will be their God, and they shall be my people." (Ezekiel 37:26–27) // "Then the Lord GOD will wipe away the tears from all faces, and the disgrace of his people he will take away from all the earth, for the LORD has spoken." (Isaiah 25:8) // "And the ransomed of the LORD shall return, and come to Zion with singing; everlasting joy shall be upon their heads; they shall obtain joy and gladness, and sorrow and sighing shall flee away."(Isaiah 35:10)

I could continue. There is the tree of life. We are told that God is Alpha and Omega, the beginning and the end. There is a river of life. There is this image of the lamb that is mentioned both in Revelation and throughout the Hebrew Bible, but then the image of the lamb is remixed into a symbol of a lamb that was slain, an image to guide the church's own understanding of its role in the world as nonviolent, peaceful, and suffering.[33]

In figure 1 is a list compiled by Wes Howard-Brook from Revelation 18, exposing the threads that are woven together to give us the critique of the economics of empire.[34]

So why does this matter? Why is John weaving together all these threads, all these images, drawing on his tradition and his past?

For a first century believer like John, history and tradition were essential to his identity; he drew on it in order to pay homage to it, in order to respect it, but also to build upon it.

He is showing the people in his community—people who are well aware of these back stories and texts—that their tradition actually gives them direction on not just how to survive, but how to undercut and subvert empire. John is claiming that all of the weight of their tradition comes to bear on this moment, that they can be faithful, even radically so.

This viewpoint is foreign to many of us living in the West today. Tradition is a bad word for some. Others seek to be spiritual but not religious. Religion itself is frequently portrayed as old, dated, obsessed with meaningless routine. Some try to live as if they have no history. Others do what they can to escape the past rather than square with it (let alone build on it). But like it or not, we are a composite of tradition, history, and context.

Consider the history of slavery and of Jim Crow in the United States, a country that portrays itself as the land of the free and as a defender of democracy. Consider also that the laws today continue to hurt people of color, making the poor suffer while the rich get richer. This is a central part of our history and of our present as well. But just as there is a history of racism and genocide, there is also a history of resistance. Claiming to be a person with no history or tradition is to ignore the injustices that people on the margins have had to face in order to survive. Claiming to be a person with no history or tradition is to also miss all of the ways people have resisted injustice. We must resist the tendency to detach from history, from the land and from the water, from the traditions and from the stories that, for better or for worse, have shaped us.[35]

We are regularly reinventing ourselves, starting over with a clean slate, but remix reminds us, just like the picture of Dylan's album, that we do have histories. We are rooted in particular places, and even the land has experienced trauma. We are made up of many threads, woven

Table 16
ECHOES OF HEBREW SCRIPTURE IN REVELATION 18

Revelation 18	Hebrew Scriptures
"Fallen, fallen is Babylon" (18:2)	Isa. 21:9; Jer. 51:8, 49
It is the place of demons and foul birds (18:2)	Isa. 13:21-22; 34:11-15; Jer. 50:39
All the nations drank her wine (18:3)	Jer. 51:7
"Come out of Babylon" (18:4)	Isa. 48:20; Jer. 50:8; 51:6, 45
Her sins go up to heaven (18:5)	Gen. 11:4; Jer. 51:9
God remembered her injustices (18:5)	Exod. 2:24
Repay her double for her deeds (18:6)	Isa. 40:2; Jer. 17:18
"A queen I sit, and I am not a widow, and sorrow I shall never see" (18:7)	Ezek. 27:3; Isa. 47:7-8; cf. Zeph. 2:15
In one day will disaster come (18:8)	Isa. 47:9
The kings of the earth (18:9)	Ezek. 27:33; Ps. 2:2; Isa. 24:21
The smoke of the city (18:9, 18)	4 Ezra 15:44
They will stand from afar in fear (18:10)	Ezek. 27:35
The traders of the earth will weep (18:11)	Ezek. 27:36; Isa. 23:8
(Cargo list) (18:12-13)	1 Kings 10:21-29; Ezek. 26:12; 27:12-24
Everything you own has perished (18:14)	Ezek. 26:12; 27:27, 34
Captains and sailors stood far off (18:17)	Ezek. 27:29
"Who is like the great city" (18:18)	Ezek. 27:32
And they cast dust on their heads (18:19)	Ezek. 27:30; also Josh. 7:6; Job 2:12
A great millstone cast into the sea . . . (18:21)	Jer. 51:63-64
The sound of harpists, musicians, flautists, and trumpeters are heard no more (18:22)	Isa. 24:8; Ezek. 26:13; (the imperial and local cults will be silenced!)
The mill, the lamp, the bridegroom and bride are no more (18:22-23)	Jer. 25:10

Figure 1: from Wes Howard-Brook

There are at least 38 references of pre-existing material being drawn into this new unmasking of the economics of empire by John.

together into who we are, AND God is making all of this new.

So John doesn't just simply make Revelation a "covers" album. He doesn't simply quote the tradition and leave it as unchanged as possible. Instead, John weaves these old threads into a new song, a new Revelation about God and about God's people who are being crushed by empire. John shows that their tradition is alive, relevant, and able to help them understand the times.

And what is this new thing?

John tells his people (here in 21) living under the Roman empire in the first century that God's holy city is coming down right in the middle of that Roman city. God is dwelling with you in the midst of all of the pain, suffering, and oppression. You are called to be faithful even when you are being crushed. Be that holy city and a light to the nations. Come out of empire. Reject the practices of the imperial religion that lead into adultery. Have no illusions. Don't be duped by the emperor's sorcery. Be that alternative community—the multitude—that rejects the beastly economics of the empire, and follow the lamb that was slain. He will lead you to life and victory. This is happening right now, right here. You don't have to wait. God is with you now. Now is the time of victory, so live as though that reality is here.

In the End, the Beginning

I want to end this book where I started it; just as Revelation itself ends at the beginning, with a tree of life in a garden and God dwelling with God's people.

We began with a sense bafflement. Personally, I am challenged to lean into the things that baffle me rather than simply rely on my old ways of thinking.

There are many questions from Revelation that still baffle me:

What does it mean for us to live as a community that is a counter-story to empire? How can we live non-violent lives that act in every situation in ways that honor our own as well as others' souls? How do we live out our own worshipful practices in ways that create something new in the world? How might we live in ways that reject the economics of empire, as we work to bring an end to oppression and poverty everywhere?

Queries

I wonder what has been important for you in this process of learning?

- How might we enter into our Christian story in deeper ways so that we might continue to create, or begin creating, our own remix that reveals and unmasks in our time the things that John was concerned about in his time?

- How might we live into the reality that God is already dwelling among us, that our imaginations are no longer marked by death or fear, that Jesus has overcome both death and fear, and that we have all we need right here before us to be the kind of church we are called to be?

- If Revelation is a Dylanesque self-portrait of the early church wrestling with its texts and stories, trying to make new meaning out of the world and understand what it means to be the people of God, then what is our self-portrait today?

God is not yet done. We are invited to enter the story and to make it our own, not simply to cover the old songs or to throw them all away, but to create new and beautiful music for those around us to hear. This invitation is always open. The door Jesus stands at never closes.

> "Come." And let everyone who hears say, "Come." And let everyone who is thirsty come. Let anyone who wishes take the water of life as a gift.
>
> (Revelation 22:17)

And in the End

Over the last century, the book of Revelation has lost its edge in the West. What was understood as a letter written to small faith communities surviving the threat of Roman empire, propped up by its imperial religion, economics and violence, has largely become a book underwriting what some have called "evacuation theology." In my view, these are two incompatible readings of Revelation.

The latter view is about how to get out of here: here often is construed as "this life" or "the world about to come to an end," but could also be avoiding difficult conversations, uncomfortable or even dangerous issues arising within a particular community. In this reading, the faithful are ultimately uncommitted to seeing the powers and principalities of this present order changed, challenged, or subverted. In this view, Jesus' teachings on the Sermon on the Mount are too idealistic to be formative practices for everyday life.

On the other hand, the former reading of Revelation reminds us that God is opposed to empire and the practices of religion, economics, and violence that it generates to sustain itself. In this space, the church is to be a brave space, bearing prophetic witness against empire. Jesus' vision of the church is designed to be a dynamic, revolutionary presence within this current order, demonstrating, what Quakers call "gospel order." Quaker testimony is born out of the leadings of Christ as present teacher, a conviction that suggests Jesus' teachings are not only practices with ongoing usefulness in the here and now, but that they are ultimately in opposition to the way of empire.

If the way of empire is about benefitting the few at the expense, exploitation, and oppression of the many, then the way of the lamb that was slain is a subversion of all of this. It symbolizes God's counter vision. The way of the lamb that was slain is rooted in nonviolence. It is radically present to the needs of the disenfranchised in our communities. It does not scapegoat, and it loves both enemy and neighbor. This reading of Revelation calls the followers of Jesus to be what African-American Quaker Bayard Rustin named "Angelic Troublemakers." Radical love through radical presence—a vision of the church we desperately need today.[36]

Afterword

C. Wess Daniels, "white male, cisgender, heterosexual," author of *Resisting Empires: The Book of Revelation* grew up "in a working-class family." His mother and stepdad "both dropped out of high school." Because Daniels shared early on the lens through which he reads and interprets the Bible, I am inclined to trust him. The reader must trust the author if he or she is going to be guided through unfamiliar and rocky terrain. And we all know that the book of Revelation is foreign and treacherous territory.

This book has given me authority to use my contextualized hermeneutic as a practical theologian and pastor. I confess that the book of Revelation had been pushed to the margins of my preaching and teaching throughout the tenure of my ministry. However, Daniels has pulled back the covers of misinterpretation and has given the book of Revelation back to the people to whom it belongs—the multitude. Daniels is unapologetic and unashamed while declaring that the Bible is a "collection of stories of poor people uniting across difference to build a social movement and winning." Knowing that the book of Revelation is for the multitude, Daniels writes and structures the book accordingly.

Daniels, a teaching professor in the best sense, writes with a plain style that captures emotional truth, and he knows his audience. Throughout the book one reads painful and honest truths: "We are victim and victimizer"; "Revelation reveals that poverty, slavery, and exploitation of the earth's resources are not a sign of a broken system"; "We need things to baffle us." It is this kind of plain talk that Daniels uses to heal the wounds from the damage the "Bible and specifically, the book of Revelation has caused." Although Daniels uses plain talk, he does not try to simplify the complex. He is aware of the multi-layered impact of empire. The book of Revelation, according to Daniels, is a resistance text for "Angelic Trouble-makers," who must learn how to remix, understand how scapegoating functions, recognize the shaping and forming powers of liturgy, and discover the composition of the multitude.

As a pastor I was most fascinated with Daniels's discussion of liturgy and community. As a preacher who pastors persons whose religion emerged from the bowels of slave ships and under conditions of chattel slavery, I must be concerned with what shapes and forms my parishioners. I cannot reproduce the content and context that enslaved black people, but Daniels has my undivided attention when he asserts that "we should think of liturgies as those practices, rituals, language, and symbols that shape us in particular ways and for particular ends." Daniels—with great emphasis—warns the reader that the empire has its own liturgy that "dulls the senses and forms a kind of alienation over time that keeps people from challenging" the status quo. Too often Black church liturgy deadens parishioners' judgments and affirms that what has always been done should continue. As a result, the Black church is often as oppressive as its oppressor. If the Black church is to be an agent of liberation, she must check her liturgical demeanor. Daniels informs the reader that there is a resisting liturgy in the book of Revelation that he calls the liturgy of *the lamb that was slain*. The liturgy of *the lamb that was slain* is based on non-violence, love of neighbor and enemy, and understands that God is the creator of all. What is clear from Daniels's discussion concerning liturgy is this: used negatively or positively, liturgy can heal or hurt, enslave or set free, either lynch people or dismantle systems of oppression. The Black church cannot afford to promote or produce any form of liturgy that does not set the captives free. There is no side stepping when it comes to how church folk are being shaped and formed. At all times, churches and culture are fashioning persons through liturgy. In other words, no matter how long we have been doing it, if it does not liberate, we can no longer practice it, ritualize it, or symbolize it. We must stop the madness. Daniels would say, no more scapegoating; stop sacrificing your freedom.

Secondly, I was captured by Daniels's discussion regarding community. The word *community* appears in this book over sixty times. Make no mistake, Daniels is concerned about this structure called community. Sometimes he speaks about binding individuals together as people, and at other times he uses language like "a thick system of relationships" to describe community. Regardless of what he calls or how he describes the community, he believes that those who suffer and are marginalized must be brought to the center of the human family. Again, I acknowledge my bias for Daniels's work. I pastor a people who have historically been pushed to the periphery of existence, even ontologically declared as non-human or three-fifths human. Therefore, to read the "multitude is a beautiful tapestry woven together of all humanity, with those who were lynched, those who were oppressed and victimized, at the center with the lamb. This centering of the victims and marginalized is something that is too often missed within western, white, middle-class Christianity today," makes my soul happy. Daniels's prophetic claim places Black people at the heart of God. Furthermore, this affirmation of dispossessed people acknowledges that true freedom, whether physical or spiritual, must always depend on those who have endured and overcome some form of oppression. Daniels's proper interpretation of the book of Revelation has given the disinherited and crucified people a weapon to fight the good fight against the empire. In *The Age of Anxiety*, W.H. Auden wrote,

"We would rather be ruined than changed

We would rather die in our dread

Than climb the cross of the moment

And let our illusions die."

Resisting Empire: The Book of Revelation destroys all illusions of the empire and empowers persons of the good book to change and not be ruined by human inventions. In summary, Daniels has convinced me that I am "already, always, been on the inside of the multitude, surrounding the lamb of God."

—Rev. Darryl Aaron

Endnotes

1. James Alison, *Undergoing God: Dispatches from the Scene of a Break-In* (New York: Continuum, 2006) 45-46)
2. Ibid., 1.
3. T. Vail Palmer, Jr, "Early Friends and the Bible: Some Observations," *Quaker Religious Thought* 26/2 (1993), 44.
4. "Cultivating the Imagination: A conversation with Eugene Peterson," by Jeffrey Overstreet, October 22, 2018, spu.edu/voices/articles/cultivating-imagination-conversation-with-eugene-peterson.
5. Elisabeth Schüssler Fiorenza, *Revelation: Vision of a Just World* (Minneapolis: Fortress Press 19091) 7.
6. Ibid., 11.
7. Ibid., 12.
8. Ibid,
9. Nancy Duarte, *Resonate: Present Visual Stories that Transform Audiences* (Hoboken, NJ: Wiley, 2010).
10. Lawrence Lessig, *Remix: Making Art and Commerce Thrive in the Hybrid Economy* (New York: Penguin Press, 2008) 76.
11. T. Vail Palmer, Jr, "Early Friends and the Bible: Some Observations," *Quaker Religious Thought* 26/2 (1993), 44.

12   Daniel Berrigan, *The Nightmare of God: The Book of Revelation* (Eugene, Oregon: Wipf & Stock, 2009) 4.

13   Miguel A. De La Torre, "Scripture," in *Handbook of U.S. Theologies of Liberation*, ed. Miguel A. De La Torre (St. Louis, Missouri: Chalice Press, 2004) 97.

14   Eugene Peterson, *Reversed Thunder: The Revelation of God and the Praying Imagination* (San Francisco: Harper One, 1991).

15   Wes Howard-Brook, *Come Out My People: God's Call Out of Empire in the Bible and Beyond* (Maryknoll, N.Y.: Orbis Books, 2010) 4.

16   Anthony Gwyther and Wes Howard-Brook's commentary on Revelation titled, *Unveiling Empire: Reading Revelation Then and Now* (2005).

17   As I reflect this I ache for so many people who have been harmed, enslaved, spiritually, emotionally or even physically abused by Christians using Revelation in any way other than one shaped by the humiliating and powerless image of a lamb slain as the one for whom God chose to represent God's own nonviolent imagination. The lamb that was slain is truly an "angelic troublemaker" to use Quaker and Civil Rights Leader Bayard Rustin's words.

18   See "Scapegoating" on wikipedia.

19   To learn more about "the scapegoat mechanism" look into the work of Rene Girard, especially his book *The Scapegoat* (1989).

20   For more on this see James Alison's, *The Joy of Being Wrong* (1998).

21   Anthony Gwyther and Wes Howard-Brook, *Unveiling Empire: Reading Revelation Then and Now* (Maryknoll, N.Y.: Orbis Books, 2010) 4.

22 Ibid., 211.
23 James Alison, *Undergoing God: Dispatches from the Scene of a Break-In* (New York: Continuum, 2006) 45-46)
24 Howard Thurman, *Deep Is the Hunger: Meditations for Apostles of Sensitiveness* (Richmond, Indiana: Friends United Press, 1973) 20-21.
25 Vincent Harding on creating the Quaker community that does not yet exist—https://www.afsc.org/friends/vincent-harding-creating-quaker-community-does-not-yet-exist
26 Elisabeth Schüssler Fiorenza says that there are three basic possibilities for 666—most scholars believe either a) it was a numeric spelling of the name Nero, b) it was a numeric abbreviation of Domitian, or c) it was an exaggeration of the number 6 which means imperfection.
27 A must read book on these issues, especially as they relate to passages within the Bible is by Liz Theoharis, *Always with Us?: What Jesus Really Said about the Poor* (Prophetic Christianity Series" (2017).
28 Elisabeth Schüssler Fiorenza, *Revelation: Vision of a Just World* (Minneapolis: Fortress Press, 1991) 87.
29 Cf. Ched Myers, *Watershed Discipleship: Reinhabiting Bioregional Faith and Practice* (2016)
30 She is a Union Theological Graduate who I met during "The Bible as Strategic Response to Empire" weekend and has a brilliant masters thesis on Revelation 13, which I read as background work for this chapter.
31 All of this should help the reader rethink what Jesus meant in Matthew 22:20–22 when he said "Render unto Caesar what is Caesars..."

32 This is not a free license to appropriate anything and everything. A critical and sensitive approach must be given to what is being used, it must always be done in conversation with others, with the proper permissions, and one should never appropriate the work of marginalized communities.

33 For instance, the image of Jesus from chapter with a sword hanging out of his mouth, feet of bronze, etc. is complete remix (based largely on texts referenced from 1 Enoch).

34 Wes Howard-Brook, *Come Out My People: God's Call Out of Empire in the Bible and Beyond* (Maryknoll, N.Y.: Orbis Books, 2010)

35 I have been thinking more and more about the work of Ched Myers and others around what they call "Watershed Discipleship," which argues that our lives are spiritual formation ought to be formed by the watersheds we live within. For a really great introduction to this topic listen to the Re-placing Church podcast with Ched Myers found here: https://www.replacingchurch.org/64-ched-myers-on-watershed-discipleship

36 This was first run as a part of Northwest Yearly Meeting Peace Month Reader in 2016.